STRONG FAMILY
STRONG CHILD

STRONG FAMILY
STRONG CHILD

THE ART OF WORKING TOGETHER
TO DEVELOP A HEALTHY CHILD

Barry Bricklin, Ph.D.
Patricia M. Bricklin, Ph.D.

DELACORTE PRESS, NEW YORK

BY THE AUTHORS OF

Bright Child—Poor Grades

Contents

Part Three: FROM BIRTH TO TEEN-AGE

Introduction

Strong families produce strong children. Although we can think of a few rare geniuses who came from disorganized families, productive and happy personalities typically emerge from stronger families.

What is a strong family? A strong family is one that is organized, not chaotic. Organization means each person knows his duties and discharges them—and knows and respects his limits as well as those of fellow family members. Patterns of communication are relatively clear in strong families: there is little of saying one thing and meaning another. A strong family is one in which each member maintains a feeling of *emotional* togetherness with fellow members. (This is togetherness in its true, not its superficial physical sense.) It is more than mere mutual concern. It is, in each member, an awareness of, and appreciation for, the family's uniqueness: the alive and vital qualities that make it different from all others. It is a conviction *not* to live at the psychological expense of others.

This unique force burns steadily in strong families, but can flicker or even die in other families. Where it flames brightly a family member derives strength from it no matter how far away he may live from the rest of the family. Where it is weak the family disintegrates, regardless of physical closeness.

Family strength is more than the mere summation of individual strengths within the family. Although each member contributes to it, positively or negatively, the product is something more—a "something" from which family members can make lifesaving withdrawals as well as deposits. A strong family is a source of increased strength for all its members.

In *Strong Family—Strong Child*, we show that parents can best deal with their children's problems—mild as well as serious—when the family structure is solid. For although only some children's problems seem obviously a result of family tensions—as when a child becomes anxious immediately after his parents have had a violent argument—there are actually a host of others, from school fears to sleep difficulties to antisocial behavior, that are also caused or sustained by family conflicts. Our aim is not to prove that all individual problems are caused by the family, but rather that a unified family approach is more effective in reducing difficulties than are other methods and can produce far more lasting results.

The quest for a strong family begins when the basic pillars of the structure, mother and father, are willing to take a close look at themselves—not with a sense of guilt, not with a sense of blame—simply as two married people. The first job is to reduce not only obvious marital conflicts but also the subtle hairline cracks that eventually sap a family of its strength.

This reduction in conflict is best achieved when each mate has gained some insight into the intense pressures to which he or she has been subjected since marriage, pressures usually below the surface of awareness. You will be surprised at the number of negative forces even healthy families have had to endure.

The first section of the book details these pressures, setting the stage with an account of how families unknowingly cause and sustain problems. It then goes back to the starting point of the process, the marriage itself, and details the largely unrealized inner psychological changes that take place. It goes on to outline what happens as children arrive and family responsibilities increase. The section concludes with concrete suggestions for unifying the top of the structure—the marital relation.

Part II, in suggesting a positive program, begins by outlining the impact parental adjustments have had on the children. The family approach is then detailed. It consists of four basic strategies or foundation skills, plus a regularly held council.

Part III gives numerous examples of the system in use for specific ages.

The system is effective and safe for children of all ages and with all kinds of difficulties—neurotic, hyperactive, uncontrolled, provocative—as well as for children not suffering any major or obvious disabilities. It can, with only minor modification, work in the family headed by a single parent and when one mate has been initially unwilling to cooperate.

While some of the explanations are given in Freudian terms, the major aspects of our system are not psychoanalytic. So we hope the book is not labeled "Freudian" either by its friends or by its critics. It is not that we disagree with psychoanalytic theories—as a matter of fact we think those on the genesis of disturbance are wholly or mainly valid. But while some of our explanations may sound psychoanalytic, the techniques are not.

The following individuals contributed to this book, either directly through ideas, or indirectly through a point of view . . . an approach.

Michael Halbert, executive director of ISIS, the Institute for the Study of Inquiring Systems; Dr. James D. Page, Professor of Psychology, Temple University; Dr. Zygmunt A. Piotrowski, Professor of Psychology at the Thomas Jefferson University (the Jefferson Medical College of Philadelphia); Dr. Van Hammett, Professor and Head, Department of Psychiatry, the Hahnemann Medical College of Philadelphia; Dr. Herman Belmont, Professor and Head, Section of Child Psychiatry, Hahnemann Medical College; Dr. Ruth Stekert, physician and friend.

The following individuals read portions of the manuscript and made suggestions, some of which were incorporated in the text and others used as a spur for better presentation: Dr. Sheldon

Rappaport, President of the Pathway School, near Norristown, Pa.; Dr. Bernard Cooper, clinical director of the Matthews School, Fort Washington, Pennsylvania; Gerry Schatz, director of the Matthews School; and Ed Dubin, psychologist in private practice.

Some of the ideas in this book were initially presented to the staffs at the Parkway Day School, an offshoot of the Institute for Learning, Child Psychiatry section, Hahnemann Medical College, and the Valley Day School for children with learning and adjustment problems in Yardley, Pennsylvania. All of the personnel at these two schools asked good questions and made useful comments, especially Joseph and Dorothy Hirt, the talented husband-wife team at Parkway Day School, and Mrs. Sylvia Heyman, educational director of the Valley Day School.

Gloria Lavenberg not only attended to the fantastic number of technical details required to prepare this book but kept a careful eye on the development of the ideas. Jeanne Bernkopf, editor, helped sharpen some of the central ideas and contributed immeasurably to the clarity of presentation.

And lastly, we must mention Dr. Jules C. Abrams, colleague and friend, who yelled at us for not having mentioned him in another of our books. (We further admit that Dr. Abrams, director of the Parkway Day School, read portions of the manuscript and made some very sensible suggestions.)

This book would not have been written at all were it not for the thoughtful questions and kindly attitudes directed at us by members of our radio and television audiences. To them we owe the greatest debt.

HUSBANDS AND WIVES: THE FAMILY CORE

PART ONE

HUSBANDS AND WIVES: THE FAMILY CORE

Ties to the Past

The United States Census defines a family as two or more people who live together and who are related by blood, marriage, or adoption.

A family has many functions. It provides for sexual satisfaction, procreation, and for the care, feeding, and training of the young. It affords companionship and a way of expressing and receiving affection. A main function of the family has always been to prepare children to assume meaningful places in society.

Many scholars who consider monogamy the best arrangement so far devised would like to prove that it represents a high-water mark of human interaction. They speculate that humans at one time traveled in hordes, led by some big daddy who had first choice among the women. From this beginning point there was supposedly an evolutionary march upward to the current peak of monogamy. But this is a difficult theory to prove since there have been monogamous arrangements from the beginning of recorded history. Most sociologists today feel that whatever family structure prevails will be the one which best suits the needs of the time and situation.

J. K. Folsom in *Sexual and Affectional Functions of the Family* claims our current social arrangement is greatly influenced by the fact that we live in a competitive, industrial society, one in which there is great emphasis on being efficient and on learning skills. There are few elaborate rituals such as mass community dances, since the time that would be spent on these rituals is spent instead competing for money.

A man has to be able to change jobs to take advantage of better opportunities, and so our culture requires great mobility. As a result, there is little emphasis on extended families—on frequent or significant interaction with distant relatives. There is, instead, a great emphasis on independence, though it results in little continuity among the generations, and little chance to pass along knowledge about children.

Nevertheless, the family itself may be considered the most important social grouping humanity has so far produced. And it is doubtful that this will change for some time to come, if ever.

The family is the source and recipient of our strongest emotions. Although we do not realize it, the people we most want to impress are our fellow family members, and they are also the people from whom we most fear criticism. Our greatest intolerance is reserved for family members. Minor offenses, stupidities, and annoyances—things we would overlook in others—enrage us when committed by our child, sibling, or, especially, parent.

The individual who has the greatest difficulty with his family is the person who has the most irrational dependency needs: excessive desires to be on the receiving end of concern, support, and affection, along with a keen desire that someone else take ultimate responsibilities. Such an individual is not only intolerant of his fellow family members, but harbors extremely mixed emotions of love and hate as well. For a person becomes most agitated when he is forced to deal with those on whom he would most desperately lean. The more our fellow family members upset us, the more we "need them," from a psychological standpoint. A truly healthy, independent person can relate with love and warmth to relatively healthy family comembers, and can separate with tolerance from those with whom it is impossible to have a relation, either because of sickness, spitefulness, or incompatibility. A dependent, conflicted person can neither separate from nor approach fellow family members.

Fellow family members conspire to lock or trap each other in certain *roles*. A role is a crystallization of some of the ways a person thinks, feels, and acts in relation to those among whom he is responding. A person may or may not be aware of the role or roles he plays; others may be far more aware of them than the individual himself. A role is the end result of pressures arising from many sources. Most important are the psychological forces at work within a family, for the family is the source of pressures least open to conscious inspection.

The pressures within a family can produce intensely negative consequences, for they may be highly inconsistent. Fathers may demand certain things of their children incompatible with the things demanded by the mother. The mother's demands may be inconsistent not only with those of the others but also among themselves, as when she demands her husband be the leader of the family and yet omits him from important decisions.

The way family members lock each other in their respective roles, good and bad, can have tragic consequences. A mother may desire a certain child to remain dependent and helpless and may create this role for him. A father may unconsciously trap his child into a defiant, "bad boy" role so that the child will express toward society the angers the father himself fears to express. The father can sustain the child in this role, by showing amusement at the child's "cute little ways" or by failing to take corrective steps. Consciously, the father may be angry at the boy for being bad, and not realize he is feeding and nourishing the defiance.

FAMILY-CAUSED PROBLEMS

A sizable number of professionals have recognized that family members indeed act (wittingly and unwittingly) to lock each other in definite roles, some positive like leader, hero, comedian, intellectual, and others exceedingly negative, such as dope, drunk-ard, complainer, uncontrolled one, bad one.

There are many reasons for this. Some explanations stress psychological economy factors: it is, unfortunately, easier to deal with people after they have been labeled or pigeonholed than as the unique, ever-changing process-entities they actually are. Other explanations are based on more subtle psychological factors, some of them simple and easy to agree with, and others more complicated and difficult for the lay person to verify.

One simple reason a parent may encourage a child in negative behavior—such as defiance, inefficiency, bed-wetting—is for exoneration: the I-was-that-way-myself factor. Suppose a mother is upset because one of her children continually fails math. She asks her husband for aid. He says, "What are you upset about, dear? I was no good in math when I was a kid." And he believes this simple explanation is sufficient. Actually, he may wish to overlook the problem for many reasons—perhaps from fear of admitting to *any* problem, perhaps to sustain the child's problem.

Another simple explanation of family role-giving is that if a sibling inherits one of the *scapegoat* roles—"Ted's the dumb one in the family"—all the other siblings want to help him keep it in order to assert their "superiority" by contrasting it to his supposed inferiority.

Or a parent may wish to prove a point by having a child maintain a negative position. A father may want to show his own father that he rears tough kids. A wife may so resent her husband's ways as to *want* her child to stay "sick" so the husband can be blamed. A husband may want a child to remain defiant to prove his wife is too lenient. The list is endless.

Attempts to destroy or weaken the relationships among others are exceedingly frequent in neurotic families. The strategies are endless: a child may repeatedly request permission to do something favored by one parent and feared by the other to weaken the relationship between the child and the rival parent; a parent may side with the child against the other parent; a child may react cooperatively with his father but uncooperatively with his mother, so that the father can express amazement that the mother is having such troubles with the child; one parent may give extra gifts to a particular child in order to seduce him; a wife may command her husband to hit a child and then soothe and comfort the child afterward to make the father seem the tyrant.

A child not only seeks to draw closer to one parent by widening the distance between the two parents but often seeks to keep his fellow siblings down for the same reason. A child may suggest "naughty" ideas to a less-controlled brother or sister to get the latter in trouble.

One of the most frequent reasons a parent may sustain weakness in a child is to keep that child in a dependent, relatively helpless position. Some parents feel useless unless they are able to command or manipulate a child. Other parents may sustain conditions of helplessness in their children as denials of their own hostile impulses. Still others are lonely. The list is as extensive as the techniques employed. A detailed account of the overly protective mother can be found in our book *Bright Child—Poor Grades* (New York: Delacorte Press, 1967).

Frequently, a parent, say the mother, will assume a role she once played in her own family, a role she cannot relinquish, either because she loved it too much, or because she hated it but unconsciously must reestablish it to resolve it. An example of the former is the mother who refuses to grow up: she wears teen-age fashions and wants to be a "pal" or "sister" to her children. An example of the latter is the woman whose father terrified her when she was a child and yet sexually excited her: she may unconsciously force her husband to assume the role of "tyrant" for her sexual and masochistic excitement and then seek to humiliate him by undermining him—in order to gain mastery of her fear of her father. Rhona Richards was such a wife. She behaved irresponsibly with the family checkbook and then accused her husband of despotism when he was forced to comment. She belittled his lack of cultural attainment, hit him on occasion, and told him he was a bad lover. At times she responded to aggressive sex on his part, and at other times was revolted by it. By this behavior she was attempting to reestablish and thereby solve the relationship she once had with her father. But since she was not aware of what she was doing and since her solution was wrong, final resolution had to await successful psychotherapy.

Sometimes a role is established by unvoiced messages. Every person sends unspoken messages, and every person receives them. Children are particularly responsive to these messages. A parent may convey one message to a child with words and quite another without them. Joseph Somers continually told his son Ralph how important it was to do things well. But Mr. Somers criticized all Ralph's work, the good as well as the poor, and as a result Ralph lost confidence in himself as an achiever. Mr. Somers had fooled himself into believing he wanted Ralph to be successful, when in fact all or most of his behavior resulted in the boy's never developing full confidence. The father's conscious or spoken message was "Be perfect." His unconscious or unspoken message to Ralph was "You can never do anything that will really please me."

Similarly, Mrs. Morgan claimed her teen-age daughter Barbara's careless, babyish ways were revolting; yet Mrs. Morgan insisted on waking Barbara in the morning, nagging her throughout the day, and filling her with advice and admonitions. The mother's spoken message to Barbara was "Grow up!" But the unspoken plea was "Don't grow up, for without you I'd have no purpose in life!"

We have seen that often a family contains a main or preferred "scapegoat": the bad one, the wild one, the stupid one, the babyish one, the "undependable" one. But it is important to understand why the scapegoat accepts the negative position. Again, the answers range from the simple to the complicated.

A simple explanation is that the scapegoat usually has no conscious awareness of what's really going on, particularly if he's a young child, and thus does not know how to fight against those patterns which have laced him into the scapegoat role.

Then, too, strange as it may seem, various pleasures are derived from having a definite role, even though it is a negative one. For example, as bad as the role may be, it is at least definite: the person caught in a negative role may not like himself but at least he knows who and what he is.

There are elements of safety that reside in the role of scapegoat. In the earlier example, teen-ager Barbara Morgan not only brought satisfaction to an important aspect of her mother's personality by acting dependently but also avoided responsibility and kept herself in the role of "protected baby." Some theoreticians would link this element of "safety" to the masochistic pleasure that can be derived from negative roles.

Finally, the scapegoat, at least partially liking his trapped position, *helps to* sustain himself in it. Since one's role can only exist in relationship to another—there cannot be a "winner" unless someone explicitly or implicitly agrees to be a "loser"—the scapegoat is part of the same game as are his co-conspirators. If a man adjusts to life by deciding he's a poor soul who needs much help and pity from others, he must also maintain the superiority of these others to gain their protection: one cannot assume the role of "protected slave" unless someone else is elevated to the role of master. In such ways do scapegoats consciously and unconsciously maintain their own negative images, though one should not carry this too far. In our opinion, it does not explain all aggressor-victim interactions, such as between armed thief and victim or murderer and murdered.

2

Psychological Meanings of Marriage

When a person marries, he changes his *identity status*—the way he thinks about himself, the sets of thoughts, feelings, and attitudes he harbors toward himself. These are the sets of attitudes that define or assign a psychological position in life.

Very few people are clearly aware of what "defines" them as people. The inner definition may be in terms of the relationships they have with parents—"I am John and Lucille's son"—or with siblings—"I am Ralph and Mary's brother." Or it may be in terms of occupation—"I am an accountant." At a less conscious level it is done with relation to remote relatives. The sense of identity is further arrived at in terms of relationship to religion and to friends. It is defined in terms of competencies, those things at which a person believes himself efficient, or in terms of incompetencies, liabilities. It may include obligations and plans.

All of these attitudes, thoughts, and feelings yield a certain overall feeling as to who the person is, where he is, where he is going, what he stands for, what is meaningful to him, which things will bring pleasure and which pain.

Some aspects of a person's identity may be trivial and unimportant; for example, his way of dressing. Such aspects can easily be changed with no danger to the overall structure or the person's mental or emotional balance. But changes among other aspects—the imagined degree of competence, degree of worthiness, or the relationship to the parents—can vastly affect the whole structure.

Marriage disrupts the identity status by causing a shift in the relationship between a person and his parents—not necessarily outwardly, in the actual relation, but inwardly, among the ideas he has of himself and his parents. Actually a number of shifts occur with marriage. Each mate can no longer think primarily in terms of being a son or daughter and so loses much psychological protection. Before marriage a person may think of himself in the basically passive position of child. A child can expect to "get" things and be protected from ultimate responsibilities. With marriage, this changes. The person is no longer only someone's child. His new identity status demands he be a giver, not merely a receiver.

Stresses and pressures which may have been tolerated with ease under old "protective cover" identity patterns (son, daughter), may suddenly emerge as threatening or panicking under new identity patterns (potent male or female, provider, competitor). For example, the idea of holding down a job may have been easy for the person who thought of himself as basically a lad with no real responsibilities. But now he is supposed to be a man. He must provide a house or an apartment; he must care for and protect a wife. He gains new privileges as well as demands with marriage (although under conflicted conditions the privileges may be experienced as demands). The right to have sexual relations is the most important privilege, for it vastly changes the nature of the unconscious psychological relation to the parents. And a married person is considered more of an adult than unmarried peers of the same age. The married person is offered a new respect; more knowledge is attributed to him. Other married people will share confidences with him, feeling that he can now understand. Other psychological changes involve the manner in which he relates to his old friends and to members of the opposite sex, other than his wife.

Marriage brings bigger psychological jolts than is commonly realized, and a good bit of inner work must be done to form a new equilibrium: a new inner relationship with the parents is needed, and consequently a new relationship with the self. If these changes cannot be coordinated into a working, acceptable arrangement—a new identity status—the individual may be said to harbor sticks of psychological dynamite awaiting a fuse.

In addition to the changes in identity status, marriage sets other processes at work. Each mate brings to the marriage a set of secret psychological expectations. Each may expect the marriage to accomplish a great deal, as though marriage could somehow be a magic solution to old problems. Typically, each person expects the marriage to give him what he lacked through childhood. A child deprived of parental affection may expect and unconsciously demand mountainous amounts of affection as a married adult.

And the expectations may be quite inconsistent. A person may demand affection at one level of the personality, and yet be unable to accept it at another level. This puts all kinds of contradictory demands on the mate.

A person who as a child was dominated may with marriage expect endless amounts of freedom, but again, unconsciously, the picture may be more complicated.

In addition, some people expect that marriage will cure them of irrational fears. A man who fears he may be homosexual may expect his newly married state to convince him—and the world —that he is not. Such a tactic may work for a period of time.

All of us to some degree expect marriage to make up for the traumatic things that happened to us—or what we think happened to us—as we grew up. This puts a fantastic burden on the marriage.

MYTHS THAT PLAGUE MARRIAGE

Many of the ills that plague modern marriages stem from assumptions that may have been valid in an earlier age and/or in a different culture, but no longer apply. Modern man knocks his head against a wall trying to live up to old-fashioned assumptions or to wished-for idealizations, myths that have never been questioned.

One of the old-fashioned assumptions concerns the assignment of power within a marriage. In earlier times, when the roles of men and women were vastly different as were the ideas of what was acceptable in a marriage, often the woman's power was inferior to her mate's. Today, it is almost mandatory that power be equally distributed.

Bhagavan Das in *The Science of Emotions* demonstrates the importance of power. Who has the greatest ability to move the other farthest with the least movement of his own? He who occupies the position of superiority. When two people interact, there is always some awareness of this power. When a boss calls an employee, the power differential can be seen physically. The boss merely moves his lips, "Jones, come into my office now." The employee must now move his entire body. This is a clear indication of superiority. The power differential can be seen in other ways. When a husband announces to his wife that he intends to see other women whether she likes it or not, and she accepts it although she is hurt and feels oppressed, there is a clear indication of superiority. The husband occupies the position of power. He has the greater power to hurt his mate. He has the greater range of movement. He can use this power to limit her behavior, while leaving himself freedom.

In some lopsided families the children come to hold greater power than their parents. By throwing tantrums, refusing to eat, or threatening to run away, a child can blackmail his parents.

Should a husband desire his wife a great deal more than she

does her husband, then he is a potential blackmail victim. Should the wife decide to carry any argument, no matter how small, to its extreme and threaten to walk out, her husband will have to give in. The husband may not even realize the problem. He may know only that he is trapped somehow in a desperate, untenable position. No matter what the cause of the desire-to-possess—love, dependence, or anxiety—if the desire is not equal, at least one partner is doomed to a life of tension. Often the first job of a marriage counselor, then, is to forge a balance of power between warring mates.

It is not always easy even for a professional psychotherapist to bring about a balance of power between mates, for the trapped one may harbor an unconscious need to be dominated. The mate who senses or knows he occupies an inferior position in the marriage must do everything possible to lift his confidence level and try to attain equality with his partner.

Romantic love is one of the idealizations that cause trouble in marriage. Too many married folk assume that the passionate "love" which characterized their courtship days has an important relation to the type of deep-seated respect and caring that gradually emerges in a relatively mature, balanced marriage. Should they discover that this romantic love has lessened or disappeared, they may think they have a bad marriage. But the presence of heady, consuming, passionate love in the early days of courtship and marriage neither guarantees nor rules out the possibility of this more mature caring attitude.

Actually, wild romantic love is usually a sign of unfulfilled longings in the person who harbors it rather than a function of the mutual relation. Theodor Reik argued in *Of Love and Lust* that a person is most primed for romantic love when there is a large gap between what he wishes for himself in some idealized sense and how he actually sees himself. The greater the gap, the more the readiness for romantic love. Each of the in-love partners thinks, "What a wonderful pair we make. We balance each other and make up for each other's deficiencies perfectly!"

With a mature couple, the sustaining factor in the marriage is a kind of mutual concern and respect, sometimes of passionate intensity, that grows gradually in the place of, or even in the absence of, romantic love. It is hard to define precisely what this more mature version of love is like, but we can make some points about its development. For one thing, it cannot develop "at first sight," for anything that develops at first sight cannot be based on genuine knowledge. If a girl falls desperately in love with a boy at first sight, the "love" must be based on her fantasies and expectations, not on anything genuine about him, since she knows nothing of him at first sight.

Mature love must grow gradually since it is based on an ever-increasing awareness of and respect for the *genuine personality traits* of the loved one. True love is definitely anchored in reality. If it is "mystical" it is decidedly not in the sense of being unreal. For if love is based on fantasized expectations it can be sustained only by the lovers' ignoring reality.

True and mature love develops not only as the mates achieve a profound respect for each other, but also to the extent that each is able to tolerate and accept the negative (but unchangeable) traits in the other. Such love is frequently accompanied by the deep-seated realization that one has made a wise choice and could not have done much better. As mature love develops, there is a gradual, partial incorporation of the beloved's personality into one's own self-system, so that what happens to the loved one comes to evoke much the same set of thoughts and feelings as would apply to the self. This *mutual* incorporation leads to the loved ones' caring for each other as for themselves. True love like this in a pure state is rare, and is somehow easy to recognize. It makes a profound impression.

But too many married partners assume this feeling of caring and concern is an external act of grace—something that just "descends" on certain lucky couples and eludes others.

This is far from true, for one of the critical determinants of mature love is the commitment on the part of one or both partners to bring it about. Love, like anything else, depends on *prior commitment*. It does *not* merely happen. Many conscious decisions must foster it, nourish it, and sustain it. And these decisions—like any decision—must be made to work.

As psychologists, we often sigh to ourselves when an engaged person speculates aloud as to whether his marriage will work. For we know that so much will depend on what he does, on the decisions he makes, on whether he will help his mate when she has erred instead of blaming her.

Whether or not your marriage will work does not depend on fate—it depends in large part on *what you will do to make it work.*

Marriage relations require effort to sustain. Many a husband goes to a party and spends a lot of time fantasizing about how a certain girl there would look and feel naked. Does he ever put such effort into psyching himself up in relation to his wife? If his wife gains weight or loses her appeal, does he ask himself, "How can I help her *want* to improve?" Or does he grow silently resentful and in his noncaring way allow the relationship to deteriorate even more? A man may be the life of the party with perfect strangers, and yet not bestir himself to make even simple one-line jokes when dining with his wife. What a stupid misinvestment of energy! Later that night he is going to sleep with his wife, not his crowd of acquaintances.

Great marital and social pain springs from a belief which is often accepted without question, that romantic love entitles the bearer to do anything in its name. How many unfaithful partners have excused themselves by saying, "I was in love! I couldn't help myself!" A person who falls in love often seems to think he and his partner have achieved some miracle that entitles them to all kinds of special sanctions. We do not claim all affairs are bad psychologically and/or morally—though we do feel that so-called experts who glorify them, typically harbor many contradictory assumptions—but we do claim that falling in romantic love is no miracle, can be brought about at will under a variety of conditions, many of them negative and neurotic, and should not be considered as a sanction which approves anything that may follow.

An unannounced affair is at least in part an act of hostility by one mate against the other. We know of no secret affair that was not purchased at the psychological expense of the duped mate. True, the duped spouse may be a displeasing partner; true, the affair may sustain a family that *perhaps* would fall apart without it; true also, the victimized mate may be better off in having at least some companionship rather than loneliness—but it is perhaps a higher truth that the duped person should have some conscious choice in determining what is best.

THE BEGINNING OF MARRIAGE

A certain pattern runs through marriages, particularly in the early stages. Because each newlywed expects the marriage to constitute a magical rebirth, there is a tendency to revert to childish ways, to indulge and to be indulged.

Not too long ago we visited some newly married friends. As we approached the front door, we could see through an open window the scene inside. The newlyweds were feeding each other dinner. We watched for a minute or two. Later in the evening we commented in somewhat astonished (though hopefully polite) tones on what we had seen. Our friends seemed surprised. One of them asked, "Doesn't everybody do it?"

In marriages which turn out healthy, these childlike needs are integrated into the continuing demands of family life. Where the changes in identity status do not rock the boat, new responsibilities are accepted as they come, and the mates still have the capacity for childlike behavior on occasions. They may romp in bed, make faces, crack jokes, act silly—when appropriate. But in couples with conflicts, one or both mates may be unable to accept the dependency needs of the other.

Most affected by changes in identity status is the individual raised on too many explicit or implicit contradictions ("Mommy wants you to be independent"; "Mommy can't stand it when you leave her") or on too many irrational commands ("Daddy hates you when you're aggressive"). Such an individual will not develop a flexible sense of identity that can tolerate the shifts caused by marriage. If, for example, a man felt implicitly commanded by his parents never to act aggressively, he may find it hard to abandon his identity as "child" and assume the one called for by marriage. If a woman had a mother who herself was unable to provide in the usual maternal sense, then the woman, upon marriage, may be unwilling to assume the role or identity status of giver. She may instead cling to the role of child, still hoping to force her own mother to be more of a mother. She has not, in a sense, solved her old identity, and hence is not free to accept a new one.

In some cases, identity changes engender immediate pain and disruption in the marriage. In other instances, they merely place the dynamite in the structure—the dynamite that receives its fuse with the arrival of children and further marital responsibilities.

There are three basic difficulties that underlie many of the problems to be found in marriage: fear of too much success; inability to accept an appropriate sexual role; intense passive-dependency needs. All three problems contain common elements and may indeed be variations of a common theme.

THE FEAR OF SUCCESS

Sigmund Freud is generally credited with the discovery that some people cannot tolerate success and are indeed frightened to death by it. A few others probably noted this strange or paradoxical aspect of life as well. In 1575, Girolamo Cardano wrote that he had a custom which surprised many of his friends. He needed a malady. He could not tolerate success without pain for too long a time, for without the pain he became terribly depressed. He fashioned a plan of biting his lips, twisting his fingers, and pinching the skin of his left arm until he cried. With this self-punishment he found he could live without depression.

It is probably difficult for people who do not know of this phenomenon to believe it exists. Sigmund Freud felt the answer was to be found in the solutions to certain oedipal situations. Each person goes through a phase in which possession of the parent of the opposite sex is desired intensely. Hostile feelings are directed at the parent of the same sex. A successful resolution of this situation is one in which the boy, for example, abandons the hope of possessing his mother and takes solace in forging a strong identification with his father, with the eventual hope of finding a female for himself. A boy who has not resolved this situation may forever equate in his mind the idea of success with the idea of committing some sort of sin against his father (i.e., possessing his mother) for which he will be punished terribly. And so, a man's fear of success may be based on a fear that success is equivalent to unleashing the omnipotent wrath of the father. Such a fear in a woman is based upon equating success with stealing from the mother that which was rightfully hers. To make this explanation more accurate, it should be added that *each success is equated with a present and active desire* to direct hostility against the parent of the opposite sex.

In some cases, continued success is equated with giving up a child's identity status. This sacrifice may be considered dangerous. In still other cases, success is feared because each progressive step involves increased (and unwanted) responsibilities.

Regardless of whether or not one accepts these ideas on the possible origins of the fear of success, the fear itself does in fact exist. Psychotherapists' files brim with cases in which massive troubles began *following* some marked success.

Michael Martin awaited his discharge from the service. He and his wife had refrained from making plans because of an uncertain future. When he was discharged, in his words, he had "everything to look forward to." He obtained an excellent job. His boss liked him. He and his wife decided to wait no longer to have children. But with everything to look forward to, Michael suffered the first of a long series of anxiety attacks which bordered on panic. He was forced to stay home from work, give up his social life entirely, and eventually to seek professional help.

Seymour Scott was a student in his junior year of college. Ever since his early school years, in which he had done excellent work, his level of performance remained in an average range. After a one-session consultation with a therapist, he found himself feeling more productively inclined than ever before. He began working furiously. He received straight A's in all his courses for the first time since those early years. This state of affairs continued for six or seven months. But he began experiencing feelings he described as "peculiar." The initial elation turned more and more to apathy. Eventually he was unable to study. He finally returned to finish up the therapeutic job he had begun earlier. His system could not tolerate continued unmitigated success.

The victims of a success fear are always baffled. They don't understand why in the world they should feel anxious with so much to live for.

When the fear of success is intense, not only is the individual in trouble, but so is his marriage. Since he cannot tolerate success for any length of time, a need to be unhappy sets in. A need for self-torment overcomes him although he usually does not see it for what it is. Just as Girolamo Cardano in 1575 had to twist his lips and pinch his arms, our modern man in trouble must flog his psyche or that of his mate.

It is not uncommon for a marriage to hold together very well during the early struggling days when the mates have common goals which they pursue together. But when success begins to set in, the husband may become haunted by the fear of it. He may work additional hours on his job and turn more and more from his wife, to deny that he is in fact experiencing any happiness and/or success. So the wife finds herself more isolated from her husband than she was during the early, struggling days. It is not uncommon then for the blade to fall after many years of marriage, when the fear of success has made itself known.

INABILITY TO ACCEPT AN APPROPRIATE
SEXUAL ROLE

A marriage may fall apart because one of the mates may be unable to assume the appropriate sexual identity status. By this we do not mean to imply there is only one type of masculine role and one kind of feminine role and that respective mates must fit these predetermined roles. A man's proper role is determined not only by his sex and personality, but by the type of personality and expectations his wife harbors. A man may be unmasculine to an outside observer but quite masculine enough for himself and his wife. Still, in our opinion, the male-female relationship is not infinitely malleable. Some writers seem to insist that any sexual arrangement is healthy and satisfactory—that, for example, the man may assume all the traditional feminine roles in a marriage—so long as both partners agree on the arrangement. We find this hard to believe. It may be satisfactory, but it certainly stretches the notion of health quite a bit.

In any event, for the sake of simplicity, let us talk about a masculine role and a feminine role.

There are a good many reasons why a man may be unable to accept the masculine sexual role in life, and there are also reasons why a woman may be unable to accept the role for which she has been biologically, psychologically, and culturally prepared. Each, as we have seen, may link successful sexuality with sinful possession of a parent. And there are other reasons. For example, a husband may be unable to accept the aggressiveness needed to carry out successful sexual intercourse. Another man may handle all interpersonal relations in highly aggressive terms, and so he may infuse sexual intercourse with more aggression than is by nature part of it.

A wife may cooperate in sex only in the early days of marriage. As her responsibilities accumulate and she finds herself unable to accept the identity status of a mature, sexy woman, she may find herself unwilling to cooperate with her husband in sexual activities. If, in addition, she resents her husband's masculinity, she will subtly put him down at every opportunity. She may insult him in front of friends, encourage the children to disobey him, be completely passive during the few sexual encounters which do occur (hoping he will interpret her reaction as his failure). The ways are endless.

Great trouble is in store for the person who, though inwardly unable to assume an appropriate sexual role, still goes through the motions of acting out the role since he or she is emitting exceedingly contradictory information. Let us use a man in our example. His overt behavior may seem totally masculine. In fact, he may attempt to compensate for his basically passive orientation by putting on shows of great strength. His wife may admire this manifest strength. But as the marriage continues and responsibilities accumulate, she will see more and more that the strength was not real. Her husband may run from decisions and in times of emergency leave the action to her. For what he actually prefers is the passive role in sex.

His problems stem less from the "femaleness" of his behavior than from the fact that he *misrepresents himself continuously*, both to himself and to his mate. Thus, at one level he promises his wife he will be a tough, virile, effective decision-maker, and at another he manages to leave this role to her.

INTENSE PASSIVE-DEPENDENCY NEEDS

Some adults have strong needs to assume a childlike position in order to be on the receiving end of affection, approval, support, direction, and especially *freedom from ultimate responsibilities*. Such passive-dependent people are not lacking skills. They can carry out the duties required of them. They are not easy to recognize by their surface behavior. At times, they may appear independent and strong. But inwardly they want to be under someone else's watchful eye and protection. They cannot tolerate a full acceptance of an adult's potent, responsible role.

Once married, a passive-dependent person expects to make countless demands, though he does not realize this consciously. Men are often adept at hiding passive-dependent impulses behind a show of strength, just as they may mask a basically feminine orientation behind this same facade. The husband may act the role of a Tarzan before marriage. His wife, who usually is more open about her dependency needs (since women are allowed to have them in our culture while men are not), is delighted to have a husband with such great strength. But, as the family responsibilities of marriage increase, the husband indulges his dependency needs. He shows himself unable and unwilling to shoulder family responsibilities. He may be so frightened of having to assume the role of the stronger one that he is unable to acknowledge any illness in his wife; he expects her, even when sick, to discharge her usual obligations without complaint. On the other hand, when he is sick he will take to bed and expect to be hand-fed.

Those with intense passive-dependency needs—especially women—may be given to extramarital affairs. They constantly seek the childlike love, benevolence, and protection that was either denied them in their own childhood or given to them in manipulative, seductive overabundance. Traditional family and household responsibilities sadden them and make them anxious. And so they ardently seek relationships in which they can indulge in a good deal of mutual babying. The affair is a perfect answer for them. It is without difficult responsibilities. The woman just concentrates on thinking of new ways to please her partner, so that she can be babied in return.

Another common method of handling unresolved dependency needs is through psychosomatic symptoms. By getting sick a passive-dependent person seeks the constant attention and benevolent support he cannot find other ways.

It is a particularly sad situation when both husband and wife have intense passive-dependency needs, for then the household usually splits apart as both mates prove unable to shoulder family responsibilities.

The fear of success, the fear of accepting an appropriate sexual role, and intense passive-dependency needs are not always discovered in a pure state. There are three common negative situations which may occur soon after marriage that reflect the simultaneous operation of all three problems. One is that either or both of the mates may be unable to shake loose of parental domination. Sometimes the newlywed's parents will not let go, sometimes the newlywed himself will not let go. If we could have the proverbial nickel for each case we have encountered in which one or the other of the mates blamed marital friction on the mother-in-law ("She calls every day"), we would indeed be wealthy. This is commonly a difficulty associated with the new wife. Her husband may complain, "She has to check every damn thing with her mother."

Similarly, the husband may manifest the same underlying problem by his overzealous desire to hang on to his old friends.

The third situation that causes tension among newlyweds occurs when the husband remains overly married to his work—or actually *intensifies* his need to work. It is a common complaint of many wives that their husbands work too many hours. This by itself does not necessarily jeopardize a marriage. But when the husband's overworking is due to a pathological inability to muster appropriate emotional reactions to his mate, we deal with a potentially serious situation. The husband may discharge his sensual, sexual, and affectional needs on his job while the wife finds herself on the receiving end of nothing. Hence, it is when the pattern is based on neurotic conflict or fear that we deal with a potentially disruptive situation. The *amount* of time a husband and wife spend together rarely determines anything important about their relationship; the *quality* of the shared time is all-important.

So it is that when a married individual cannot accommodate identity changes, a crack is opened up in the structure of the marriage. As we have seen, three changes are particularly hard to accept: the image of oneself as a continuously happy, successful person; the image of oneself as a potent member of a particular sex; the identity change from passive-dependent child to adult personality.

3

The Impact of
Children on Parents

THE FIRST CHILD

Up until the time the first child arrives the married couple could
very well remain in the "honeymoon phase." True, all of the
many changes in identity status mentioned previously have taken
place. True also, the wife or husband may be overly dependent
on mom; the husband may cling to old friends and old ways; the
husband may remain married to his work. But it is still not uncommon for there to be no negative results seen or felt during
the early days of marriage. When the first child arrives, however, a
great many further psychological changes occur. Again, the identity changes may not be readily apparent. And as with everything
else, the impact may be greater on certain individuals than on
others, depending on the degree of preexisting vulnerability.

The child will produce the most negative impact within people
who are highly immature, secretly dependent and who themselves
still wish to be children.

Theoretically, one would expect mothers with great maternal

drive to be more receptive to new children than mothers with less maternal drive. However, the whole idea of a basic maternal drive is difficult to deal with, since there are no ways to measure it directly or even to prove it exists. Even if it does exist, it must immediately interact with a number of other personality forces, some good, some bad. In our opinion, there probably is a basic maternal drive, but it has little explanatory value.

With the arrival of the first child, there are profound inner changes in the basic identity status of both husband and wife. A child is major evidence that one is no longer merely someone else's son or daughter. This is most significant. So long as one imagines himself solely in terms of being the child of another, he may imagine or fantasize that there is magical protection available to him, that no matter what responsibilities come along he can always, so to speak, "return to his parents." This is *somewhat* changed by marriage, but *grossly* changed by the arrival of a first child. This is one of the most basic identity changes imaginable, for, in a sense that will never again be matched to the same degree, the husband and wife are truly responsible for the life and well-being of another life. Even the surgeon responsible for the life of his patient, the airline pilot responsible for his passengers, the teacher responsible for her class do not experience the same psychological feelings of responsibility as those felt by the new parent.

Sometimes this responsibility is not felt all at once. There is the excitement of the new baby to mask the immediate impact. Or, in a longer time sense, the new mother may still feel herself under the omnipotent protection of her own mother. But sooner or later the "scary" impact will be felt. People who are essentially conflict-free, or whose problems lie in other areas, gradually assimilate the impact of the identity change with no trouble.

Things are not quite so easy for those people who must still imagine themselves to occupy the child position in relation to their own parents. Such people cannot tolerate the image of themselves as parents able to give, provide, and protect. To the highly dependent childlike individual, it is a shock to envision the parent role.

Another basic and profound change in identity comes with the arrival of a child. A person who is able to produce a child has proof, living proof, that he is a powerful and potent sexual adult who can do the same wonderful magical things his parents have been able to do. Some people welcome this entrance into the truly adult world. Others resist the implied change. Still others are panicked by it. A parent in conflict may see in his child proof that he has competitively outclassed his own parents by producing a being deemed superior.

The seeds are set for a most serious problem when the mother unconsciously expects her child to make endless demands on her. She may act in an overly indulgent manner toward the child, attempting to appease his imagined insatiable appetite. Or she may so resent the imagined drain as to become completely rejecting. Both reactions make things worse, to the point that the mother's fears become a reality. The fear of being drained tends to grow worse as the years progress and marital responsibilities increase. But, typically, the fear has its inception with the first child's birth.

Insecure fathers are particularly threatened by the arrival of male children. This is part of the Freudian oedipal complex: the father sees the newly arrived child as a rival for the mother's attention and favors. The father might not realize it and might not say anything about it, but inwardly he is threatened. He resents the amount of time, love, and devotion the mother gives to their son. Unconsciously, he may retaliate by deriding the child. Or he may become intensely demanding of his wife: "You never seem interested in *me* anymore." Of course, to the extent that these charges are *true*, we are dealing with a mutually disturbed pair.

We hasten to point out that not all of the psychological changes associated with the first child are negative. If they were, no sane person would ever want to get married or have children.

So for the moment let us concentrate on the positive psychological changes that come with the first baby.

Aside from the many obvious joys children bring—they're cute, fun to hold, watch, and play with; they make a house feel lived in, and they exude life energy—children also seem to satisfy some deep longing for immortality on the part of the parents. Almost everyone fears dying to some extent and would like to leave tangible evidence of having existed. The child constitutes such evidence. If this need can be handled in such a way that the child is not overly manipulated, the result is a healthy situation.

Furthermore, not every aspect of the identity status of the parent is bad. For the first time in their lives, the new parents will be able to understand their own parents. There is no feeling that duplicates the love of a parent for a child. No child can understand this attitude of caring until he or she has children. When children complain how much even healthy, nonmanipulative parents lean on them, it is because they are as yet unable to understand what they mean to their parents. As a matter of fact, they would probably be neurotic if they did. For children want and need independence and are not equipped to understand parental concern.

After all, children come into their parents' lives long, long before parents come into the memorable consciousness of the children. The parents were, so to speak, always there, but by the very same token, not there at all. Children are aware by their second or third month that someone or something is out there, but they do not have a clear perception of what it is. The infant has no idea how cute he is and what feelings of love he produces in his parents. And so the older child is never able to understand why his parents are so concerned about him, because he does not realize what his presence has meant to his parents over the years. It is only when he has his own children and realizes how much he cares for them and how strongly he wishes well for them that he is at last able to understand some of his own parents' reactions. Then there can develop a bridge of child-to-parent communication far greater than any that could have existed before.

AS FAMILY RESPONSIBILITIES INCREASE

As some years pass and there are more children to provide and care for, more financial burdens, the inner stresses intensify. We demand more of ourselves as our stations in life rise. We demand more accomplishment on the job. And we demand more of ourselves as parents, community participants, citizens, and responsible relatives.

Then come the tragedies common to those who have experienced stresses which could not be accommodated by their revised identity patterns, tragedies involving those three areas of difficulty: fear of success, inability to assume an appropriate sexual role, and intense passive-dependency needs.

THE WOMAN WHO WANTS PANTS

Some women are, consciously or unconsciously, resentful of what they assume to be men's greater power in the world. Other women had fathers who were either too autocratic or too weak. All these women may end up with one thing in common: a need to pretend their husbands are the strong and dominant partners in the marriage, along with a simultaneous desire to prove this is not so.

Such a woman *talks* as though her husband were the boss, but she gradually takes over every power function within the family. On the surface, the husband may seem quite pleased with what he describes as his wife's efficiency or strength. And perhaps part of his personality, a dependent part, *is* grateful. But another part of him may cry out in indignation.

The wife sometimes resents the fact that she is left holding the bag in all emergencies and is expected to solve all crises, major or minor. But she really has no intention of relinquishing her role of power. This type of dominant, overbearing mother typically goes along functioning quite well and only occasionally breaks down and complains bitterly of her lot in life. She usually pulls herself together in a short time, and once more grabs the family reins.

THE HUSBAND WHO ABDICATES

It is not uncommon for a husband to crumble gradually under accumulating masculine, fatherly, and job-related expectations. He may already have had a strong fear of success or of a fully masculine orientation. Perhaps he feels he cannot live up to his own expectations. As his responsibilities increase, so do all the proofs that he is no longer a child. He may have what is popularly called a nervous breakdown and not be able to go to work. He may find himself anxious and/or depressed around the home. He may insist his wife accompany him places and be at his side to help him lest he be overcome with anxiety.

The wife will probably be unable to handle the crumbling masculinity in her husband and will usually react in one of two harmful ways: she will either take over for him and thereby force him to feel all the more impotent, or she will turn angrily away from him, complaining he is no man. Alternatively, she may look for an affair with another man or develop a whole host of complaints of her own.

THE FUSSY HUSBAND SYNDROME

Some husbands attempt to hide their anxieties over the identity changes of marriage by denying their masculinity and usurping the feminine role. The whole drama begins innocently enough. The husband babies his wife. Saying it is enough that she looks appealing, he proceeds to take over most of the household functions. He explains he is more efficient than she. He may be, but by grabbing the reins he prevents his wife from gaining efficiency.

At first she appreciates her husband's interest but gradually she becomes anxious and/or depressed and cannot tell why.

When they have children, she begins to resent openly his fussy ways. He may or may not resent the fact that he is stuck with so many family responsibilities, but he will accuse her of being disinterested in the home.

The wife may suddenly fall out of love with her husband, though still unable to put her finger clearly on what bothers her. What neither of them realizes is that they are both battling to possess the female role. Their situation is doubly complicated if the wife is herself mixed up concerning the role she would like to have.

This situation typically requires professional help.

THE AUTOCRATS

Some husbands fear being affectionate and may play at, or actually be, hard, ruthless businessmen. They may become autocrats at home. Their reactions are often based on very deep, intense fears of passive feminine tendencies. The stronger the fears, and the less equipped the person to acknowledge them, the greater the problem.

Marriage and family life call upon a man to act occasionally in a compliant manner. But the autocrat cannot tolerate such demands. He may insist his house be run with the ruthless efficiency of his office. He may horrify his wife by beating the children.

This man needs help badly, but typically will not seek it, as he despises weakness, and cannot admit a need for help which he equates with weakness.

MARQUIS DE SADE

Some men develop sadistic orientations toward their wives. The sadism may take the form of beatings, but more typically manifests itself via sarcastic mockery, accusations, unfair behavior, and extreme passive-aggressiveness. The sadism may be more extreme when the husband is drunk.

This type of situation generally requires professional help, since the pattern is often based on a very confused relationship between the man and his seductive mother. If, however, the man happens to marry a woman who is masochistic, their marriage may endure without the need of outside help. But, for some reason, truly masochistic women are either very rare or are not really attracted to men like this.

More typical is the wife who is fascinated with a masochistic role for a few years and eventually becomes fed up. The marriage usually falls apart after some seven to twelve years. The wife may complain to a therapist that her husband has been sadistic all along, but that she hoped he would change. Her own masochism —what is still left of it—shows in that she set her husband up with unconscious provocations.

THE MAN BREAKERS

Women who had ruthless or impotent fathers often turn into wives who resent any form of masculine authority. Their goal in life is to emasculate men. The following case is typical.

In the early years Ella put her husband Thad on a pedestal. She looked up to him in every respect. But as time passed and Thad could not live up to Ella's irrationally high expectations, she became disenchanted and then gradually hostile. Her hero had feet of clay.

Ella became sarcastic and sought to rob her husband of his

position as main decision-maker within the family. The situation worsened when he began to drink, proving Ella's hypothesis that he was no good. At this point, Ella sought professional help— not for the sake of her marriage but because she was worried about her children.

A variation on the man-breaker theme occurs when the wife knowingly marries beneath her, with the belief that after the marriage she will gradually raise her husband's cultural level. But after the marriage, her husband sits in front of the TV set and drinks beer, just as he did before the marriage. As time passes, the wife blames the meaninglessness of her life on her husband's unwillingness to join her in cultural outings. She becomes openly hostile.

Women such as this must be shown that their lack of fulfillment is based on contradictions in their own personalities, and not on their husband's pedestrian attitudes.

Then there are the women who have deep-seated insecurity feelings and are thereby motivated to want a high degree of financial security. Such a woman is included with the man breakers because typically she uses sex to land and control her man. She continues to be sexy during the early years of marriage and seems anxious to please her husband. But her femininity is phony: her main interest is power and security. She gradually abandons any desire to please her husband sexually. She may still dress extremely well, and appear seductive when with company, but it is all a show.

There is a new type of man breaker in today's world, a woman who handles the stresses of marriage and family in a truly subtle way. She becomes intensely psychology-minded; she reads every bit of psychological advice put out. What she is really interested in is delving into her husband's mind—not so much to educate him as to prove he is the "culprit." He feels that he is under a microscope, or that he is being asked to change in ways he doesn't understand.

THE FEAR OF BEING DRAINED

Intense dependency needs in the wife may show themselves in a variety of ways. She may have a child who exhibits any number of neurotic disabilities. She herself may feel depressed and/or drained. Her husband may complain that she is unable to assume wifely duties.

What is wrong is that she has not been able to abandon her childlike position. She is unable to separate psychologically from her own mother, although on the surface she may sever all contacts; her mother may even be dead. What we mean by her inability to separate from her mother is that she is overly involved and/or linked with that parent by one or more irrationally intense needs; they may be a need for approval, justification, forgiveness, affection, support, advice, or, on the other hand, a need to hurt and destroy. Such needs can exist unconsciously, even if the parent and child see each other rarely or never.

An early warning signal may be the wife's need to see her mother with high frequency, or to avoid her with the same frequency. The overly intense needs may show themselves in a heightened sensitivity to the mother's comments. Or the wife may fear to expose her children to her mother, believing that the mother will seduce them away.

Just as a dependent woman has the unconscious need to fasten onto her own mother in an attempt to suck out imagined answers to her problems, she has an unconscious fear that her own children will make endless draining demands on her. To compensate or appease or hold off these imagined onslaughts, she forces more on the children than they really want—whether it be milk, attention, advice, or her presence. But the more she gives them, the more she spoils them, and the more spoiled they become, the more obnoxious and demanding they become. She ends up with the very situation she sought to avoid: with children who make persistent, never-ending demands.

Some young mothers at this point become terribly depressed. Others attempt to ward off the anxiety by trying to avoid wifely and/or motherly responsibilities. Some have an intense desire to return to school or to go back to work—to do anything reminiscent of the prematernal state.

We have painted an extreme picture. The syndrome comes in all varieties of intensities, from very mild and quite manageable, to very severe requiring professional help. And of course, not every mother who wants to work or return to school is neurotic. Indeed these desires may occur in the very healthiest mothers. The crucial factor is not the desire to return to work, but the reasons behind the desire.

4
Reducing Negative Emotions

Before you and your spouse can deal effectively with the problems of your children, you must learn how to strengthen your own relationship by reducing your negative emotions—hate, anger, disgust—in order to be able to communicate without intense personal blame.

When someone feels blamed for something, he erects a wall which prevents meaningful communication. He stops paying attention to the contents of messages aimed at him and insulates himself against the blame.

Furthermore, should the blaming occupy center stage for any length of time in a husband-wife relation, each mate may become perversely addicted to it. Even if only one of them actively begins to *seek* the negative emotion, the chances for reasonable settlements between them are small.

Our experience has convinced us there is a large body of people who ensnare themselves in chronic neurotic interactions that are fed by the exchange of intensely negative emotions. These interactions are doomed to endless repetition unless the negative emotions are reduced. Our purpose, then, is not to turn people into saints but to show them how they can strive for progress.

Reduced negative emotion is achieved through a general three-stage process:

1. Acquiring insight into personal and family distortions.
2. Learning to challenge and change the irrational beliefs and assumptions that cause and sustain negative emotions.
3. Learning to cope with and change stubborn habits.

It is only when these steps have been mastered that one is in a position to communicate without blame.

But the most important part of the process—and the only system that will work—is for you to concentrate on improving yourself, *not* your mate. You may want to understand your mate's negative behavior, particularly in terms of how it interacts with your own, but your ultimate aim must be *self-improvement*. Should your mate perceive your real interest as being either to change or blame him, forget about positive results.

You must start by searching for insights into the negative role or roles you may be assuming within the family—searching out at the same time the irrational beliefs and ideas that may be sustaining much of your misery: "I positively can't stand it when my son is angry!" "My husband is a dirty rat because he won't help out when he should!" Although insight alone does not change negative patterns, it is a necessary first step, for without insight, it is hard to identify those patterns that *should be* challenged and changed.

AN IMPORTANT THEORETICAL INTERLUDE

Any approach that claims people can alter their own emotions and behavior, and subsequently those of their children, by learning to think more rationally leans heavily on the assumption that negative patterns are a result of the manner in which people think about and hence interpret the world around them—and that people are not helpless puppets of fate but rather play big roles in creating the emotional climates in which they live.

We cannot go into a complete discussion of the validity of the assumption that self-defeating patterns are based ultimately on irrational beliefs. Interested readers should refer to the books of two psychologists, Magda Arnold and Albert Ellis, as listed in the bibliography.

Magda Arnold has devoted much of her life to the study of emotions. She claims that emotions do not directly follow a source of stimulation; there must be an "appraisal" or "estimative" step involved. If a person should thwart you or your child disobey you, you do not become "automatically" angry, whatever that may mean. You first evaluate and appraise the situation as being anger-worthy. It is only after this bit of rapid "evaluating" that the emotion develops. The complete emotional reaction is of course more complicated, since bodily changes take place that help to promote a cycle reaction.

Albert Ellis, too, has used this assumption to build a system of psychotherapy. Though the assumption is not new, no one has made such explicit and practical use of it as has Ellis. He explains his position in terms of an A B C sequence. Something happens in the outer world: someone insults you. This is A. We then have an emotional reaction: we become enraged. This is C. Ellis says most people would think that the angry emotion arose from the insulting remark, that C followed from A. But instead there is a middle step, B. B is how we interpret A and what we tell ourselves following A. The insult has no power to do anything to us until we interpret it. We tell ourselves something, usually in the form of sentences that flash through our minds so rapidly we may not even know they occur.

Let us suppose two people are confronted with the outer event A in which someone makes insulting remarks. Let us suppose that the first person quickly says to himself: "That bastard! He had no right to say that. I'll bash his head in." This man will rapidly have angry emotions. Suppose the second person says to himself (and most important, *believes* it): "This guy feels inferior, and thinks by attacking me he can make himself feel better." The second person may have very little negative emotion. Hence what is said (*and believed*) at point B is of decisive importance in determining the feelings and actions to follow.

The statement made at B depends upon more than an interpretation of the immediate situation. Of decisive importance is the individual's prior system of values. For example, the first person's "That bastard . . ." would have no impact on him unless he already had the idea that people who say what they have no right to say should be violently attacked. *And so in helping a person overcome self-defeating action patterns one investigates and challenges implicit and explicit value systems, not only the words at point B.*

This type of psychotherapy does not deny the existence of psychobiological factors that may predispose some people to react more violently than others. And it does not explain why some people seem to interpret their worlds more irrationally than others, nor why certain individuals are better able to challenge and change irrational value systems than are others. But it does assume that the best place to grab a rational foothold in the process is at the level of those inner sentences and the preexisting (implicit or explicit) value systems.

The self-help system presented here is based on the fact that we can *learn how to stop producing painful and negative emotions and actions by learning to reinterpret the situations which caused them, and by rethinking the philosophies in whose name they were called forth.* In the example given, the first person must decide whether the insult really constituted a danger which had to be met with counteraggression. In short, he must question his belief that people who holler irrational insults should be attacked for their irrationality. Then he must train himself to stop making false and irrational interpretations. In this way he will learn not to upset himself to begin with.

This theory *is not based*—we repeat, *not based*—on *the assumption that one learns to stifle or swallow anger.* Such "swallowing" would increase anxiety and agitation.

THE ROLE OF INSIGHT

The role of insight in a self-help book must be qualified. First, not all persons will profit to the same degree. Second, we do not believe a reader could possibly understand let alone remember all the points made in the previous chapters concerning distorted family interactions.

But if you and your spouse read those chapters, you ought to come away with the feeling, "My God, we *have* been through a lot together. Considering all that *could* have happened to us we're lucky we still talk to each other at all." Even this "low-level" insight will be helpful.

There is no question that the more a married couple can understand the pressures to which each has been exposed, the better. Not only does this insight encourage mutual sympathy—itself desirable—but it places each mate in a position to understand what negative themes should be worked on and/or eliminated.

So our aim in this section is to help husbands and wives discover what kinds of inefficient, neurotic, and perhaps painful interactions they may be caught up in.

Self-defeating patterns are in the majority of instances based on irrational or distorted attitudes and beliefs. No matter how complicated the neurotic pattern—be it the father who cannot control himself and yells at his children, or the mother who cannot allow her child to become independent—a careful analysis will show some irrational attitudes at the foundation of the problem. In the case of the yelling father, the irrational assumption may be a combination of the belief that he is in great danger when he is acting as the assertive leader of a family, and that people who annoy him by insisting he be a leader *ought to be* less pushy and leave him alone or else be castigated. The mother who cannot grant independence may harbor a number of irrational beliefs: "Without my child I have no reason to live"; "People will judge my total value and worth as a mother by how well my child can do things—and therefore I'd better keep a very careful control over him."

We have already mentioned three key irrational beliefs that wreck many marriages: "I am in serious trouble when I am continuously successful"; "I cannot safely be a sexually potent, pleasure-loving assertive adult"; "I am in danger when I can no longer think of myself primarily as a child."

As we have seen, these three false beliefs are all variations on a common theme, and furthermore are frequently never voiced consciously. A person may believe and act on these falsehoods, without clearly realizing it. A mother may irrationally believe herself unsafe because the arrival of her child has changed her own identity status from child to mother, without her ever understanding that the irrational belief is causing her troubles. Consciously, she may experience only her "symptoms": depression, a feeling of being drained, an unwillingness to carry on. But when she can confront, understand, and gradually change the irrational belief that underlies her symptoms—when she can learn that life contains many potent rewards for the adult—she will no longer have to resist experiencing herself as a mother. Should she persist in clinging to the irrational belief that it is unsafe and uncomfortable to be a giving, mature adult, she will have to resist experiencing herself as a mother and hence will have to deny her children. Should this denial itself be intolerable, the only thing left for her is despair and depression. But she will get maximal relief when she no longer believes herself unsafe or cheated as an adult.

Some irrational beliefs can be discovered (and hence challenged and changed) by simple introspection—by listening to what you are saying to yourself in your inward conversation, such as "I can't stand always having to be the responsible one, dammit!"

Others are more difficult to discover and involve learning to pay attention to your chronic or long-lasting action patterns.

Still other irrational beliefs are so woven into the context of behavior, thought, and feeling (in analytic terms, held out of consciousness by repressive forces), as to be virtually "unknowable" without professional help.

But remember, the quest for insight is a quest for irrational beliefs. Some are obvious. Others are not, and *can only be inferred from behavior*.

There are basically two levels to be considered in your search for these irrational beliefs. One is the level of what you are saying inwardly: "I must make my children obey or I'm a terrible father." The other level is a search for implicit values you harbor, often without knowing it. As we have seen, these are the beliefs in whose name neurotic behavior is summoned.

Take the person who gets exceedingly upset when addressing a group. No matter whether he realizes it clearly or not, his implicit belief system must contain elements like the following: "It is terrible to make a mistake in front of a crowd"; "I am not a man if people laugh at me"; "It is ridiculous to assume people would really want to hear me." Yet all he may consciously experience with any clarity is anxiety.

SOME COMMON SELF-DEFEATING ASSUMPTIONS

Some irrational beliefs are common to parents of disturbed (and even not-so-disturbed) children. One is particularly common not only among parents but also among teachers of hyperactive children. This belief, if completely verbalized, would go as follows: "I am to blame for the child's continued poor behavior. If I were more capable and potent as a personality, the child would not have the problem." Countless teachers and parents hurt themselves by labeling as weakness their inability to make things instantly better. Their anger may explode at the child, but they are really (irrationally) furious with themselves because they feel powerless to change the situation.

A much more sane belief would be the following: "My child has some difficulties. Perhaps I even contributed to them unknowingly. It will take a while to change things. But I ought to realize that the job wouldn't be easy for anyone at this point, and so there's not much sense in blaming myself when things don't go right immediately."

Another false or irrational assumption is common among men —the assumption that disobedience is a threat to masculinity. A man suffering under this belief irrationally assumes it is a sign of weakness when people do not listen and obey the first time he gives a command. He has identified his worth and his manliness with his ability to make people—especially his children—listen to him. When a child does not obey, he wrongly believes his worth as a man is under attack, and he responds with rage.

A woman with difficult children may feel that because she gives so much of herself to them, they *ought* to repay her with kindness and cooperation. And so she makes the irrational assumption that their negative behavior is a personal attack on her, a rejection of her love and devotion. Actually, the children may be out of control for a variety of reasons—including the desire to get even with their mother. But regardless of the reasons, she is still hurting herself by imagining she will get an even "return" for her investment of kindness. She is lucky to get even an approximate return.

Following are some of the ways you can discover what negative roles you may be playing in the family, and the nature of some of your irrational beliefs and assumptions.

1. Pay attention to your thoughts and feelings when you are caught up in stressful situations, so that you can learn to be emotionally honest. Ask yourself, "How do I *really* feel?" Do not ask yourself only what you happen to be saying out loud (often an inaccurate barometer), but what you are saying deep, deep inside. Next time you find yourself yelling at your spouse, deep down inside you may be saying, "I just can't lose an argument. It makes me feel so small. No one would respect me." Or when you are irritated at your child, you may be saying inside, "Dammit! Doesn't he realize how worried I am about him? He's not improving and I can't seem to help him."

2. At the same time, pay attention to your behavior. Ask, "How

do I *act* in such and such a situation?" It is too easy to deceive yourself by asking *only* how you feel or what you are saying. You have unconscious forces to reckon with and cannot always be aware of all that motivates you. But you can get some insight into this unconscious aspect of your personality by looking at your *typical behavior patterns*.

Suppose someone swears up and down he is not angry with his boss. Yet suppose an outside observer notices that each time the person acts in relation to his boss, he does so angrily. After three or four such observations, it would seem pretty clear that the person is angry with the boss, no matter what he consciously thinks.

Mothers of insecure children may believe they give their children endless opportunities for independence. But if they really tried to observe their own chronic and typical reactions, they might discover they rarely relax enough to allow independent behavior. They might find themselves tying their child's shoes when he could do it for himself ("It's quicker this way"), or telling him what book to consult for a homework assignment ("It would take him all night his way"), or telling him how he should feel and act in countless situations ("Why not save him the time and trouble of having to learn for himself?").

A woman who wants her husband to take a more active role in the family might notice, by studying her behavior patterns, that each time there is some family interaction she grabs the floor and tells the children what to do. But she will only discover this *if she is able to review a number of these situations and search out themes common to all of them.*

Observing your own behavior is one of the most effective ways of discovering how your current identity status may be threatening to you. Perhaps you will notice that you are often anxious *after* something successful happens, or that you seem to pick fights with your spouse just *after* some common good fortune, or that you become upset when your mate wants to lean on you and you refuse to play parent to the child that lives in him. Such indications may mean that you irrationally fear continued success, or that you irrationally believe you are being cheated and hurt by your spouse's demands. Once you have discovered these irrational beliefs, you can confront and challenge them.

3. Try to gauge the effect you have on others, not to blame yourself but to see how you are registering. You can learn much about yourself by knowing the impact you make on others. Psychotherapists make it a practice to tape-record some of their sessions for later review. It is amazing how much we learn. Many times we may have credited ourselves with neutrality in a certain situation. On hearing the tape later, we are struck first by the impact we are creating, and then by the emotion in our voices, sometimes an anger we were not aware of at the time. The tape recorder helps us discover what we were thinking at the time.

   Similarly, many families have found it instructive to tape-record dinners when the whole family is together. The taping is done openly, and after a number of runs everyone is so used to the machine that it is ignored. It is very instructive to listen to the recording a few days after it was made.

4. Listen to other people's opinions about you, instead of rejecting them. This is not to say you should take them so much to heart that you start blaming yourself. But you will have more sources of information.

5. Make a list of what you want and expect from people in your family—and make another of things you expect from yourself. Work on the lists over several days, but do not reread early items as you add new ones. Add to the lists when you are in different moods—and at various times of the day. Then, after a number of weeks, inspect the lists carefully. Be on the lookout for contradictions: "I want my husband to make important decisions"; and then a few items down the list, "Harry should consult me before taking important steps."

   You may find other pairs of opposites: "I dislike it when my son acts angry in the house"; "I wish my son would stand up for himself in fights." It may be you are expecting him to behave one way in the house and another way outside.

6. Try to be aware of the sentences that flash rapidly through your mind. Even in situations in which your anger seems to come instantaneously, try to remember the pain-inducing thoughts that preceded the anger. After you have "caught" a number of these sentences, you may discover some values in yourself of which you were unaware. For example, after you catch and line up a series of thoughts that ran through your mind as you exploded in anger at your mate, you may realize that the theme common to all of them is your need to justify your reactions, coupled with a conviction that you are somehow a failure if you cannot force your mate to accept this justification. How many wasted hours are spent by each mate trying to get the other to see that he or she was justified in some former action. Who cares? So what if your mate *doesn't* believe you behaved rightly?

CHALLENGING AND CHANGING IRRATIONAL BELIEFS

Your first aim was to discover the irrational role or roles you may have been playing in your family structure, and the irrational beliefs which undermine your behavior. Your next aim is to learn how to challenge and change these irrational beliefs. Remember, the aim is not merely to change what you are saying to yourself, but *to change belief systems.* (Some people believe that if they merely eliminate or change the actual words they are saying to themselves they are "cured." Likewise, some believe that if they unthinkingly say something such as "Damn, I'm getting a headache," they are doomed to that outcome. Those are both examples of a belief in magic—the magic of words.)

Unfortunately, changing beliefs is no easy matter. You must challenge the beliefs persistently, both during stressful periods and at other calmer times as well.

Let us consider a common irrational belief almost all of us harbor to some degree, that it is necessary for others to approve of us all the time. We first attempt to cope with it by saying to ourselves, "This is stupid; it doesn't really matter what others think." We may tell ourselves that a number of times. Nevertheless, we find that when others do disapprove of us, we still feel tense or angry. So now our agitation may increase. Not only do we still believe it is terrible for others not to approve our actions, but we now blame ourselves because we cannot shake loose of this belief. So, instead of being better off, we have added self-blame to the other troubles. We lied to ourselves; we said it did not matter what others thought, but when the chips were down we still cared.

Nevertheless, if you *persistently* challenge an irrational idea, you can get somewhere. At every appropriate opportunity, try to convince yourself that constant approval is not a dire necessity, and that should people disapprove of you, nothing serious will happen. In the beginning, you will find an immediate increase in your sense of well-being, but this feeling does not typically last long. At times you will feel less threatened by the evaluations of people, but at other times you will feel more guilty and confused than ever—upset and annoyed with yourself that you are still so negatively affected by others. *You will, then, be in a sustained period of guilt and confusion, a period in which things become better and worse at the same time.* We have found that it takes anywhere from four to twelve months for a person to convince himself even in a small (but genuine) way that the opinions of others have far less importance than he previously ascribed to them.

We cannot mention too often that success in challenging and changing long-standing beliefs does not come easily. For example, for many years you may have equated your ability to have your children mind you with your total sense of self-worth. Consequently, any time you are not immediately heeded, you may consider it an attack on your strength as a person. This belief may engender terrific amounts of anger and frustration. But it may take you a long time to convince yourself you are not inferior when your child, because of his own problems, does not obey you instantaneously.

There are a number of things you must accept about yourself before any change is possible. First, that you are a human being, and human beings are imperfect. Also, that many impulses and drives are natural to your personality. You must learn to be appropriately self-interested. You must accept that you have certain needs and the right to make certain demands. Indeed, if you cannot learn to make appropriate demands, your deep needs will go underground and create caldrons of discontent. You will unwittingly seethe with resentment and end up making truly intense irrational demands. And if you cannot learn to state what you really want, you will end up demanding what you don't want. Eric Hoffer is fond of quoting the saying that we never seem to get enough of what we do not really want in the first place!

Once you can accept these facts—that you are an imperfect human being, that you need not blame yourself for mistakes (you will make plenty), that you can never achieve a state of perfect happiness but that you really don't need perfect happiness anyway, that there are a number of basic drives which are and ought to be part of your very humanness (including anger, grief, and lust), and that it is quite permissible to state your true deep feelings—then, and only then, are you really in a position to challenge and change the irrational beliefs that have plagued your life.

Challenge those beliefs persistently every opportunity that presents itself. *Do not vow to become a perfect human.* Hope, rather, that each year will find you a little more rational than the year before.

BREAKING STUBBORN HABITS

Psychoanalysts call it working through. Behavior-modifiers call it changing habits, relearning, deconditioning, desensitization. Whatever anyone calls it, it is a long phase of trying like hell to substitute calmer and more rational reactions for inefficient, trouble-causing, anxiety-arousing, family-disrupting, efficiency-robbing reactions.

During this long phase it is extremely helpful to be painfully honest with yourself. Do not tell yourself you are making more progress than you really are. Do not tell yourself you are not angry when in fact you are furious. You might better tell yourself, "I am enraged right now. But I don't need to feel this way every time, and I can try to do better next time."

It is very helpful when attempting to substitute rational for irrational reactions to relax your muscles completely. It is easier to behave rationally in a state of relaxation, easier to substitute rational attitudes for the irrational ones when the muscles are not tense. But it is by no means easy to relax your muscles once you have engendered a great deal of negative emotion within yourself.

Different people find different strategies for relaxing successful. It is often helpful to perform some act which is not typical for you. If you usually pace when your tension mounts, try sitting down and taking deep breaths.

Try conditioning yourself to relax at bedtime, by working on one muscle group at a time. Lie down and concentrate on allowing your feet to relax. Once they are, if only to a minor degree, allow the feeling of "letting go"—which is what relaxation is all about—to move up your legs. Then relax your hips, chest, back; let it go down your arms, up your neck to your head, even to your jaw and facial muscles. You will find that each step facilitates the next. Once you have gotten into the *habit* of relaxing, you may be able to slip into a state of relaxation even when under stress.

There are other common-sense things you can do to aid relaxation and hence help yourself challenge and change irrational beliefs—a number of good mental hygiene habits you can adopt.

1. Learn to distinguish between meaningful planning for the future and rehashing of unlikely possibilities. When you're

about to meet a new and important person, deliver a speech, spend a day picnicking, or take the kids out, the statistical chances are that things will go well. But too many people spend 95 percent of their waking time hashing over the 5 percent chance that things will *not* go well. Their attitude is ultimately based on what might be called the please-God-punish-me-in-advance belief that if one suffers enough in advance the fates will capitulate and allow the coming event to go well. Stated simply, too many people believe the act of worrying about something makes it less likely to happen. It doesn't.

2. When you plan all the many things you have to do, remember that you are *not going to have to do them all at once.* Just because you can *think of them* all at once does not mean you can *do* them all at once. The projects may knock about and collide in your head giving the false impression that the reality is also going to be pressured and chaotic. In many ways, thinking is *not* an accurate reflection of reality. What in the mind may seem a hopeless pileup of pressure can in reality be dealt with one item at a time. One item at a time cannot swamp you. It is the false image the mind yields in presenting all items simultaneously that overwhelms you.

3. Therefore, learn to work on (or think about) one item at a time. People lose their ability to concentrate because they try to swallow too much at once—they apply a basically "oral" attitude to their thinking. When you work on one thing at a time, you accomplish more because you deal with fewer distractions. Your power of concentration is increased. "All very well and good," you say, "but how does one learn to think about one thing at a time." The answer is that it is not too hard if you do not harbor the irrational belief that new tasks must be accomplished instantaneously.

Whenever you find your mind has drifted from what you want it on, force it back where it belongs—by sheer willpower. Most people find it difficult to keep focused and become frustrated with each attempt. So in their typical self-defeating way *they assume they cannot do it, and give up. The trick is this: start with the conviction that you will switch your mind back to the single task at hand no matter how many times it may wander.* This conviction, that no matter what is involved you will simply stick to the plan, can carry you through. Each time your mind wanders, simply pull it back—five hundred times if necessary. Do not worry or even think about how many times may be involved. Simply do it.

Summarizing, to improve the overall strength of the family, the husband and wife must learn to reduce negative emotion. They need insight into their neurotic interactions so that each mate may realize what they both have had to contend with. The irrational, pain-producing beliefs that sustain neurotic interactions can be identified, confronted, challenged, and changed—given patience and a willingness to sustain many failures along the way.

5
Foundation Skill 1:
Communicating Without
Blame

Once negative emotions are reduced, concrete ways to improve communication between husband and wife (and thereby between parents and children) must be established.

Genuine communication of ideas and feelings is possible only if blame has not become a chronic part of the picture. Relatively mature, fairly nondefensive couples will be able to tolerate the occasional bursts of rational hostility as well as the infrequent explosions of irrational overly defensive hostility that are part of every marriage. No marriage, however, can endure endless episodes of blame-hurling without becoming sick.

We are aware of the writing that advocates marital partners be *encouraged* to fight. But the titles of these works are often misleading since, though fighting is encouraged, the rules are very special as to what type of fighting is permissible. Actually, if the mates follow the rules advocated, they will neutralize any genuine aggression or intense hostility which may have been present.

And so even the let's-teach-'em-to-fight books enforce our original point: communication is enhanced when the tendency to hurl angry blame has been reduced. Furthermore, these books serve the important function of making people feel less like failures when they *do* fight, thereby reducing guilt and self-hatred and increasing self-esteem. So the next time around they are likely to be *less* hostile to begin with. Hence, if these books wish to substitute a detoxified form of aggression for the intense, angry, blaming hostility which is so often a part of sick marriages, fine. But let there be no mistaking the central issue: the tendency toward chronic hostility must be reduced. Dr. Haim Ginott advises that it is perfectly all right to be angry as long as no personal insults are uttered. For example, if you are furious, instead of yelling personal insults you are to say, "I am full of consternation." The weakness in this approach is that when your voice is up ten decibels and your face crimson, people rarely listen to your actual words. They hardly listen to your words under the best of conditions and do not listen at all when they detect fury. Your wife burns your shirt. You remember not to scream a personal insult ("You clumsy idiot!") but instead scream: "I cannot stand to see burned shirts!" Can you now picture your wife, as she sees your red face, listens to your enraged voice, and dances to avoid the specks of foam from your mouth, saying to herself: "Oh, hark— he's not really personally attacking me. He's only bothered by seeing a burned shirt." We doubt it. Careful wording to avoid personal insult is a good intermediate step, but not an ultimate goal.

We do not say you should never get angry (as if this were possible) or should stifle or swallow anger. Such tactics make you seem either a liar or else fearful of your own anger. All we mean is that the ultimate aim is to learn gradually not to upset yourself to begin with. It is not much help to suppress your anger or to act calm when you're not or to talk in long funny phrases ("I am full of consternation") when this is not the way you feel. (Of course, such phrases may make you laugh, in which case you will feel less threatened, and under this condition, the technique serves to reduce the underlying angry emotions.)

We do not expect people to be saints. Nor do we feel that all anger is irrational. But the more mature a person becomes, the greater the likelihood that he can endure bursts of both rational and irrational aggression without needing to launch an explosive counterattack. And the less defensive he can remain, the more he helps his mate to achieve this same goal, for over the long haul, genuine improvement in one mate breeds improvement in the other. (Even minor saints make their followers healthier, not sicker.)

But when a person in psychic trouble is subjected to a relentless barrage of blame, he is unlikely to change for the better by rethinking his attitudes and beliefs.

Let's look at the entire notion of blame in our culture. Guilt is assumed to be a necessary element in the control of behavior. If a person does something wrong, it seems not enough simply to stop him and ask or force him to do the right thing. The blaming tradition seems to insist that we stop the person, *blame him*, then ask or force him to act otherwise. The act of blaming is a needless step and one responsible for much human misery.

Suppose a young child is to come in from the yard at 5:00 P.M. The time arrives, and the child makes no appearance. The parents fume. More time passes. Finally the child comes in. The parents scream at the child, making clear that he is a worthless idiot. How much easier it would have been to walk outside, take the child by the arm and say, "It's five o'clock, you have to come in." We do not mean that parents should follow their kids around and lead them by the ears. But we do mean that effective action does not depend upon the use of blame and anger. *And if a calm although firm attitude is taken when the children are young, more radical methods will not be needed when they are older and harder to control.* Firm insistence breeds ultimately a willingness to follow the rules of the game.

We are not advocating a wishy-washy, permissive system, but we are advocating one that operates as free of blaming tendencies as is humanly possible, since blame is a destroyer of effective communication and self-esteem.

As we have noted, when a person is being blamed for something, he rapidly becomes unable to pay attention to what is being said. He is receiving only the message of hostility. When you hurl blame at a person and at the same time try to tell him how his behavior could be improved, he will pay absolutely no attention to your message, except the part that says "You idiot, you are to blame for all that I'm trying to change." Blame arouses a need for revenge rather than a desire to learn and change in positive ways.

Furthermore, blame gives provocative people what they want and reinforces their negative behavior. Both adults and children may thrive on sadomasochistic interaction, and unconsciously yearn for the blame and anger that sustains neurotic cycles.

In general, blame increases feelings of inadequacy, and thereby sustains negative emotions and actions.

Now for some of the things you can do to communicate more effectively, including how to stop blaming yourself, for when you are no longer a self-blamer, you will no longer blame others.

1. Learn to differentiate between situations in which it is rational to be angry and those in which anger or blame is an exercise in futility. Rational aggression is that evoked by a threat to your physical life or to your *vital life space*, your range of essential options.

   For example, if one member of a motorcycle club insults another member in such a way that if the insulted member does not fight back he will find his status and range of alternatives (access to more desirable girls, etc.) reduced, aggression launched in retaliation would be rational. True, the insulted one can say, "Why should I fight, it is only words," but nevertheless his life *has been affected*. Aggression launched against something that would really and truly make a vital difference in your life is rational.

   This is not to say that all genuine attacks or challenges *must* be counterattacked. Even when your aggression is rational, you may decide not to respond outwardly. You may decide that counteraggression, though rational, would only make things ultimately worse. The attacked motorcycle club member may decide to accept reduced status rather than to enter a fight in which he may be defeated. In order to prevent a major war, a nation may decide not to launch counteraggression, however justified. A husband may decide his wife *is* reducing some of his options, but that out of mature consideration he prefers not to counterattack.

In everyday life, the huge preponderance of aggressive, blaming attacks are completely irrational: they are launched (or countered) *where there has been no real or significant attack.* And they are launched against actions that could not possibly affect life or vital life space. An out-of-control child, a sassy child, a screaming spouse can*not* genuinely affect either your life or your vital life space. True, they may demand *effort* on your part—you may have to set some limits—but they cannot really hurt you or your way of living, significantly. Most aggression is evoked by situations that could not possibly affect your life in any long-lasting or concrete way—*except in terms of your own irrational inner definitions.*

If you believe that it is horribly unfair of your children to bother you and of your spouse to be angry with you, you will then feel aggressive when they do. But if you do not harbor the unrealistic expectation that you can have children without being bothered or that your spouse will always be loving, you will see that such situations present no danger—no threat to your life or vital life space. Aggression, in such instances, is excess baggage.

There are some situations in which it is not always clear whether or not your life space is under attack—when the boss yells at you unfairly, or when your child throws a fit in a supermarket. But even in these the tendency is to see more danger than there is. Your job success will eventually have more to do with your skill than with anything else, and it is unlikely your neighbors will judge you inefficient just because your child fussed and fumed in the market; the same thing has probably happened to them.

2. Learn that adopting a nonblaming attitude is not the same as adopting a passive, defeatist, "permissive" attitude. Advocates of the scream-and-hit-'em school live in a two-class world: you either scream and hit, or you're weak and get walked on. But those are not the only alternatives. There are all kinds of effective actions that can be taken *without* anger and blame.

   And so, when your spouse or child is behaving negatively and irrationally, and you find yourself boiling over with rage, ask yourself, "Am I really being hurt or affected by this?" "Will counteranger, *even justified rational* counteranger, help?" "Is anger the most effective measure I can take?" If the answer is "Yes" to one or more of these questions, then go ahead and get angry. But we will bet you those occasions are rare.

3. Learn to separate cause from blame. Just because someone indeed caused something to happen is no reason to assume that he must be blamed for it, even if what happened had negative consequences. A wife who forgets the keys to the house and locks herself (and her husband) out is certainly the cause of the subsequent difficulty. Does this necessarily mean, however, that she must be blamed for her inefficient behavior?

   How about the child who *deliberately* hits his sibling, or the husband who *willfully* chooses not to phone his wife when he knows he will be late for supper? Is anger understandable in such situations? Certainly. Is it, however, worthwhile? Probably not. Is it necessary that every mistake be angrily punished? Or is it more helpful and rational to do something that will decrease the chances of the same thing happening again?

   Remember our prior warning: this is not a philosophy to adopt overnight. There will be a long period of confusion during which guilt is added to the original anger—guilt that you cannot control the anger.

4. Realize that the tendency to blame yourself and others is a habit, not a need. Though it is perfectly true that frustration tends to engender anger, and that as a group humans certainly

seem easily frustrated, this does not mean you are doomed to be angry whenever an external situation provides an opportunity. You must first define the situation as anger-worthy. If you do not, then anger is not inevitable.

We recognize that aggression is "natural" in the sense that it is one of man's inborn capacities, that it is, unfortunately, a very common response since man is apparently frustrated by very petty things, and that it is no easy matter to learn to differentiate a genuine from a nongenuine attack. We further concede that very few people will ever achieve a state in which they are *never* irrationally aggressive, and just as few will achieve a state in which they are *hardly ever* angry. Nevertheless, the important thing is to try to make steady improvement in this area so that each year finds you in slightly better shape than the year before.

5. Note carefully that *anger should not be swallowed or stifled.* The aim is to learn not to generate it in the first place.

OTHER RULES OF COMMUNICATION

Aside from learning to reduce blame, there are a number of other rules to follow for better communication.

1. Learn how to *inform* your mate of your feelings. It is indeed not only permissible but desirable to *air* your deep-seated reactions. What is not desirable is to *hurl* them. For example, suppose that something your spouse said has enraged you. No matter how you try to substitute a rational for an irrational response you find yourself extremely upset. Your impulse is to begin shouting. But we submit there is an in-between step, not so drastic as screaming your anger at your mate and yet better than standing there stewing. This step is to tell your mate how you feel. You might say, "I want you to know that I am extremely upset right now. I can't even think straight— because what you are saying has hurt me."

You may feel silly, stilted, and artificial at first. Indeed in some ways you are. But in another sense you are being genuine and honest. That *is* the way you feel. True, you would rather lash out and hurt your opponent. But to substitute a watered-down message is more helpful and is not basically dishonest, since you *realize very well what you are doing*.

This technique will enable you at least to have the measure of satisfaction that comes from informing someone else of your deep-seated feelings. You will discover how much better it is than hurling endless blame—and how much better than trying to swallow your anger.

2. When you are arguing with your mate, observe two basic rules. First, spend as much time as you can trying to understand his position: you may discover the two of you are not far apart, and you may even start your spouse learning about your side. Secondly, spend at least some time trying to figure out why you are being overly sensitive. Don't worry about beating his arguments down. Remember that very few issues are ever resolved in an angry, blame-hurling discussion anyway; finding an accommodation is much easier when anger, blame, and defensiveness do not entangle the situation.

These suggestions will certainly not solve all difficulties. There will be many instances in which you and your mate are genuinely far apart. But by using these rules, perhaps you can at least reach an accommodation before the situation escalates into a full-scale war.

It has been our observation that many husbands will maintain a nonblaming attitude for only one interaction. For example, suppose a wife does something to anger her husband. He knows the rules of communication and does not respond with blame. He may even say, "I am sorry you are upset, dear." But if this does not mollify her and she continues her attack, he then explodes, "You ungrateful wretch . . ." And the situation further entangles itself. In other words, such a husband may mouth nonblame but what he is really saying to his wife is "I will not blame you, provided you immediately fall in line and appreciate the fact I am not blaming you." If his attitude is not immediately reciprocated, he explodes.

Effective communication at the top of the structure is necessary before any serious (or even not so serious) problems can be handled within the family. If these suggestions work, patterns of effective communication will develop between the husband and wife.

But sometimes increased communication heightens the tension between husband and wife, and even leads to a chronic state of friction, because there is some genuinely irreconcilable incompatibility or highly neurotic interaction. Under such circumstances, professional help should be sought.

A FAMILY APPROACH: THE FOUNDATION SKILLS AND THE COUNCIL

PART TWO

A FAMILY APPROACH:
THE FOUNDATION SKILLS
AND THE COUNCIL

6

How Parental Patterns
Affect Children

In the preceding section we have concentrated on ways husband-wife conflicts produce hairline cracks or actual splits in the family structure and ways these splits can be recemented. In this section we ultimately develop a total family method of strengthening children. This particular chapter sets some perspective by showing how parental attempts to solve their own problems can have life-long effects on the children.

WHAT THE CHILD REPRESENTS TO
EACH PARENT

A psychotherapist generally begins his attempt to understand a mother and father's behavior toward the children by seeking to discover what secret or unconscious expectations each parent has for the child. Knowledge of these expectations can enable us to understand not only the negative impacts the child may have had on the parents but also those the parent is having on the child:

in short, how the arrival of the child may have weakened the parent—and how the parent may be weakening the child.

Each parent unconsciously sees the child as fulfilling a definite role. This can be bad for two reasons. A child may be thrust into a role whether or not he is fit for it. Furthermore, the unconscious role is often at odds with other conscious roles the parent expects of the child. When a parent has a strong need to see a child in a certain way, he will be blind to the real needs and capacities of the child and will give the child incorrect, nonvalid feedback.

For example, a father may have a need to see his son as perfect, the wonderful specimen the father himself could not be. As a result, he will be incapable of seeing the child the way he really is. The father may condone his son's malicious behavior, declare inferior performances perfect, or excuse rudeness. But usually the father will wake up some day, see the son as he really is—as the father made him—and then hate him.

Another example is the father who has a need to have an aggressive child because he deplores his own lack of aggressiveness. Again, he will be blind to the child's other needs and will set up a system by which he will demand the child be aggressive. The child, for a variety of reasons, may not fulfill that demand. But the child is in a bind, because the father communicates to him that he is only acceptable when acting aggressively. The child's mother, on the other hand, indicates that to her the child is acceptable only when he is not aggressive. This wraps a noose around the child's neck. And the noose may be tightened by the fact that only a part of the father's personality wants the child to be aggressive while another part demands docility.

There is no direct or easy way to predict from parental behavior what he or she may actually want from the child. For example, overly manipulative treatment may result from a need to view a child as an achiever, and may also result from a mother who feels she is totally responsible for everything about the child. Nevertheless, there are some common findings we can map out.

It has long been obvious to students of personality that parents *contribute* to—but by no means are totally responsible for—neurosis in their children. They do this through a variety of behavioral patterns: being *overly* affectionate, manipulative, anxious, protective, indulgent, seductive, or hostile. Or they may go too far in the opposite direction: being *underly* affectionate, protective, concerned, and so forth. The results correspond to what we know about the physical world: a live organism can suffer from not enough water or too much water, not enough heat or too much heat.

Following are some of the common patterns we have encountered repeatedly.

THE CHILD AS COMPETITION

Let us suppose that one parent, say the father, has a need to see the child as a tool of competition—a way of competing with his own parents. The father may unconsciously desire to prove he is a better parent than his own parents were. He will become overly manipulative of the child, in order to make of the child a perfect, glorious, achieving champion. And he will become overly demanding and unresponsive to the child's real needs.

A woman too may feel the need to compete by use of her child. Adela had a mother who in subtle ways as well as obvious ones made Adela feel inferior. Adela grew strongly resentful and terribly anxious to prove that she could do things not only as well as her mother but even better. When her son Francis was born, Adela immediately viewed the child as her redeeming champion. She never clearly realized she had chosen Francis for this role, but she was aware that she wanted Francis to be at his best when her mother was present, and she kept him dressed up for those occasions. Again without realizing it, she became highly demanding of Francis: when he was still very young, she insisted that he stand up and recite long poems; she demanded that he be a champion among his friends. This imposed an intense burden on Francis and at the same time filled his mother with a sense of guilt, for unconsciously she had mixed feelings about being competitively superior to her own mother.

THE CHILD AS "BOSS"

A few years back the interesting discovery was made that some parents of delinquent children unconsciously encouraged the delinquency. These parents were themselves inhibited in the expression of anger, even appropriate anger: they could not tell off the boss even under massive provocation, could not stand up for their rights. Such parents may unconsciously pick the child to be their mouthpiece by fostering aggression in the child.

Delinquent and/or aggressive behavior can be fostered in many ways. The parents may side with the child in a battle against school, where it is obvious the school personnel are in the right. They may fail to set proper limits when the child is young. They may secretly laugh when he wins fights unfairly, or acts aggressively with his peers.

Or, on the other hand, they may incessantly tell him he is no good, doomed to becoming a criminal. This is the so-called "self-fulfilling prophecy." As a result of this particular kind of treatment, the child figures to himself, "I am already accused of being aggressive; why not be just that?" Besides, the child senses, deep inside, that *this is really what his parents want and expect.*

THE EMASCULATED CHILD

Sometimes a parent has a marked fear of aggressiveness in a child. Such a parent sees to it that a premium is placed on "being nice." Even appropriate aggression is immediately squelched.

Some parents have a need to see themselves as omnipotent. They are threatened when someone does not follow orders. Such parents typically attempt to keep their children in dependent, submissive orientations.

And a child may be rendered impotent as a personality in a number of other ways. There is the case of the father who sees his son as a potential rival. James Williams was the type of father who demanded perfection in all his children, but particularly in his oldest boy, Jimmy, Jr. He was constantly correcting Jimmy, for the child never measured up to his father's way of doing things. Whenever Jimmy would show his father a particular bit of work, James would disapprove of it. When questioned about his attitude, James Williams claimed he really did respect his child's work, but thought it more important to point out the errors so it could be even better. He was strong for excellence in his child. This was the father's feeling at a conscious level, but his unconscious need was to emasculate Jim, to make him feel he could never be a full competitor.

A child caught up in a situation like this will realize his father actually rejects good performances and will therefore develop a strong unconscious need to fail. And a true neurotic bind will come to exist.

THE CHILD AS LOVER

When a mother has not resolved her relationship with her own parents, has a need to control others via love and sex, and has a tremendous fear of rejection, she may act in an overly seductive way toward her child. She may display herself to him either naked or in a state of partial undress. She may stimulate the child beyond his capacity to handle the stirred-up feelings. She means to bind the child to her with a thread of sensuality. These patterns may be especially intense if her own husband is on the go much of the time and cannot provide her with sensual attention.

When Mary was a child, her father had turned to her for much of his own sensual satisfaction, since he felt somewhat rejected by Mary's mother. He had held her too much, kissed her too often, touched sexually responsive parts of her body. Now that she was an adult, Mary was unconsciously quite attached to her father, though on the surface she often acted as though he were repulsive. She had developed a tremendous fear of being rejected and sought to control other people by making them love her. When her own child, Nathan, was born, she unconsciously fostered a seductive type of togetherness. She took him to the bathroom with her. She bathed him thoroughly, concentrating on his genital regions. She put him in her bed. She presented herself in the nude to him unnecessarily. Consciously, she reacted strongly against signs of sexual interest on his part and made him feel very guilty about the whole thing. She yelled at Nathan when he had an erection while lying with her.

Again we see the type of bind that accompanies such neurotic situations. On the one hand Nathan's mother stimulates him; on the other, she is furiously indignant when he reacts to her stimulus.

THE CHILD AS POSSESSION

There is the mother who imagines herself totally responsible for everyone within her family. This is the kind of mother who feels guilty when someone feels blue. As a result, she becomes greatly overcontrolling. She must manipulate everything that goes on within the family to make sure no one makes her feel guilty.

Related to her is the mother who unconsciously rejects her child. So intense is her own anger that she imagines the child is in constant danger. Here we are dealing with a so-called projection of the mother's own deep-seated wishes: she wishes the child hurt or in danger and so begins to imagine he is. To deny this terrible possibility, she manipulates all the child's waking hours. The child develops few genuine independent skills. At some point the child is placed in a further bind as the mother grows tired of the manipulative role and wants the child to be independent.

As we have seen in all these cases of child manipulation, one of the main dangers is that the parent is completely unaware of the real child, his real talents, and his real needs. The father who wants an aggressive son will become furious instead of supportive when his child loses a fight. This fury further scares the child, making him even worse as a fighter. The mother who has a need to seduce her child will be gravely threatened when he attempts to move off and establish some separate identity for himself. She may turn on him violently.

But once the parents understand themselves and strengthen their own relationship, the child-strengthening strategies can be put to work.

WHY PARENTS MUST COOPERATE

Mrs. Sheila Harter feared that Arnold, her first child, would hurt himself if he were allowed to play with his peers, whom Mrs. Harter had decided were too rough. As Arnold reached the age of four, he sensed both his mother's fear and how much his father resented the mother's overprotectiveness. Arnold's father felt the boy was being weakened, but kept quiet to avoid an open battle. Mrs. Harter knew that if she allowed her husband to gain control of Arnold, her own influence would be lessened and Arnold would be exposed to the dangerous world. So she undermined her husband's influence by leaving him out of important decisions. Mrs. Harter had no awareness of what she was doing. On the contrary, as Arnold became more fearful and neurotic, she complained of her husband's passivity, not realizing she herself had pushed him out of the family's inner circle.

Arnold, by this time, had grown dependent on his mother's attentions and now desired to own her exclusively. Unconsciously, he sensed he could achieve this goal by widening the rift between his parents. So he would deliberately ask to do dangerous things when both his parents were present. He knew his mother would turn him down, and that her action would cause anger and resentment on his father's part.

The bitterness became open when Mr. Harter felt himself

excluded from the family and Mrs. Harter grew more angry with her husband's seeming passivity and more concerned about Arnold's growing neurosis, a fearfulness actually engendered by her crushing overconcern.

When a family like the Harters reach a psychotherapist's office, the parents are rarely aware of all that has been going on. Their complaint is rather typically expressed, "Doctor, Arnold seems very anxious. Can you help him?"

If a situation like this is to be treated on the home front, it cannot be "cured" by any single strategy. The parents must forge a working alliance between themselves, one secure enough to prevent the child from exploiting any real or apparent parental rift and yet not so possessive as to freeze the child out.

It is well-nigh impossible to help children overcome difficulties in the absence of parental unity, for such disunity spreads downward from the parents and gradually disorganizes the whole family system. Furthermore, parental disunity increases a child's anxiety even though he may actively seek to contribute to it. And his increased anxiety adds to his overt "symptoms" which makes everyone feel worse.

Given parental disunity, inconsistencies will not only undermine discipline but will also allow subtly corrosive factors to operate. At the surface level, inconsistency breeds pessimism. Neither parent tries very hard to make a system work, thinking that the spouse does not care anyway. The father, for example, may feel, "Why set limits? As soon as I leave for work his mother lets him do whatever he pleases." And the mother may feel, "Why try to be patient with the child? As soon as his father comes home he'll begin yelling at him anyhow."

We all know the obvious ways children exploit parental rifts, as when a child asks his mother if he can go to the movies, gets a No, and then tries his father, who is more lenient, but there are more devious and dangerous ways in which parental disunity is exploited, as illustrated in the Harter family. A dependent or neurotic child often seeks to strengthen the bond between himself and a "target" person by weakening the bond between this person and all others. Hence, Arnold Harter would rub salt in parental wounds to widen the gap and draw his mother closer to himself.

On a practical, nonpsychological level, parental cooperation makes any system work better, since what one person forgets the other may remember.

7
Foundation Skill 2:
Setting Limits

Children need many limits when they are too young to protect themselves from simple hazards—and fewer limits as they grow.

Limits are needed for three main reasons: to keep children healthy and safe until they learn to take care of themselves; to aid in the learning process by helping children decide what needs immediate attention and what can be left for more leisurely accomplishment; and, perhaps most important, to end some children's intense need to provoke parents and authorities into acting angrily.

Many neurotic children and even some normal children have a need for negative emotion. This need is behind much of what is commonly called "bad behavior." A main purpose of limit-setting is to make it impossible for a child to evoke the negative emotion he thinks he needs.

THE NEED FOR NEGATIVE EMOTION

A provocative child will seek your anger, disgust, hatred, and contempt with a dedication hard to fathom. His parents will either be puzzled—"Why is he pushing me like this? He seems to *want* me to hit him."—or will scream, "You're never satisfied until I end up hitting you!"

Most provocative children push until the parents reach a breaking point. The children are aware that anger and hatred are building up inside their parents; nevertheless they continue. In the majority of instances, the parents notice only that physical punishments are ineffective.

The highly provocative child may seek negative emotion more intensely than positive emotion. Stated more accurately, the part of his personality that craves negative emotion gains the upper hand over the more rational aspects of his personality.

It is extremely important for anyone who works with provocative or poorly controlled children—or indeed for anyone who works with any child—to understand the need for negative emotion.

At the foundation of the child's need for negative attention is separation anxiety—a dread of being left alone or abandoned. This is even more basic in causing him to seek negative attention than is his obvious need to punish both himself and his parents with his behavior. Separation anxiety is not always easy to spot since it can go underground and be seen only in the symptoms it produces, from whiny demands to psychosomatic ailments to endless provocation.

The child has a strong need for your attention, your love and support, to reduce his separation anxiety, a fear that most theoreticians believe is the cause of all other forms of anxiety. But the child finds he cannot seek love and praise, either because he is guilt-ridden and feels uncomfortable when he gets it, or because he has been overly manipulated and equates love with psychological suffocation—or because he feels love is conditional and must be purchased at a price he cannot pay.

And so though he wants the positive attention to quiet his fears, he renounces it. Now he is in a bind, for he feels isolated and abandoned. Therefore, he hits upon negative emotion—your anger, irritation, or even active hatred—as a perfect solution for a variety of reasons:

1. Negative emotion forces you to pay a great deal of attention to the child. When you are irritated with someone or are screaming a punishment, your awareness is "full" of that person. Negative attention is a distorted umbilical cord between the person giving it and the person receiving it. It is intense and highly personal. It is almost sensual in quality, though only a nondefensive, keen observer would realize this. To the provocative child, negative attention is usually perceived as superior to positive attention, for the praise most parents and teachers give is far less intense than their anger and irritation. (This does not imply that a false intensification of praise will reduce a child's difficulty. Manipulative praise rarely works.)

2. Negative attention is so easy to get. It is, unfortunately, easy to make parents and teachers angry.

3. Negative attention is simultaneously its own punishment and license. The child endlessly seeks to punish himself for his inner guilts, and your anger, hate, irritation, give him endless license to continue punishing you.

4. Negative attention provides built-in protection to the child who fears psychological "suffocation." Children who have been overly manipulated, seduced, or intruded upon, want to draw very close to those on whom they have become dependent, yet fear that by so doing they will have to relinquish their own willpower. Negative emotion has two simultaneous "pushes"— toward and away from. It binds parent and child to each other, but by its irritating quality prevents a complete fusion.

Hence negative emotion cements the two into positions

neither too close nor too far apart. That would be fine if the pushes toward and away from did not build to insatiable intensities. The child and parent thus caught cannot move closer to each other nor can they back away, and because each push demands infinite satisfaction they cannot relate in a healthy, flexible way: intimate, not smothering; close sometimes, distant others. Nor can they escape the pain, for the process is unconscious and doomed to continue until the cycle is consciously disrupted.

5. Punishment is ineffective in limiting this kind of behavior, since the very threats you shout are what is sought. In short, when you scream your rage at the provocative child, you throw fuel on a fire you imagine you are putting out. The child does not actually seek to be hurt, but he does want your intense emotion to be directed at him.

The provocative child pursues his goals by seeking to be center stage in your awareness—as did Timmy in this example.

Each morning Timmy's father would say cheerfully, "Good morning, Timmy!" Timmy would say "Yecch," and make a face. The father would throw his arms in the air and walk away muttering, "What's wrong with that kid! There's no pleasing him!"

Suppose Timmy had answered his father's cheery "Good morning" with "Hi, Dad." He would have been in and out of his father's awareness in one second. But, instead, look what happens. Timmy says "Yecch," and grimaces. Father walks away muttering—and continues to mutter for at least ten minutes. Timmy has unconsciously invaded and then taken over his father's awareness for at least nine minutes and fifty-nine seconds longer than he could have with a positive approach.

The only path out of the bind is the elimination of negative emotion. If the anger is removed, the child will learn that he can live and survive without it. And his own negative behavior patterns will be reduced since they will not be reinforced.

What is required, then, is the reduction of negative emotion but *not the absence of limits.* You must learn to set limits while projecting the least amount of negative emotion possible. And note we are concerned with limits, not punishment. Punishment implies blame; blame is based on anger; anger is a negative emotion. Stated simply, when you limit a child you do just that and no more—limit his behavior. When you *punish* a child, you implicitly (or explicitly) blame and hurt him, and hence sustain his disturbed condition.

We do not claim that the mere setting of limits will eliminate a child's need for negative emotion. The ability to communicate without blame must be part of the picture. In fact, the need to set the limits nonblamingly is so important that this foundation skill might just as well have been named "setting limits without blame." You can't set limits while blaming for the same reason you can't communicate while blaming: when intense blame is part of an interaction, nothing else registers. A provocative child who feels blamed for his behavior will continue it, for he will gladly trade whatever physical punishment you mete out for a chance to upset you. Blame makes this trade fair. You may punish the child but he "gets you," as proven by your anger. When limits are set nonblamingly, there is no trade or deal. The child's negative ways win him nothing.

There is another reason why limits are more effective when set calmly. When a child sees you are upset, he knows you are worn out by the confrontation. And he also knows that when people are worn out and at the end of their ropes, there is a good chance they will do anything to finish the confrontation, *including surrender*. Hence your agitated anger sends this message to your child: "Continue the assault—I am about to surrender."

The provocative child must move within a firm environment that will not oblige him by yielding large amounts of negative emotion.

It is a widely noted fact that provocative children are often extremely ambivalent. This means they often want to do something and not do it at the same time. Very often they become tearful and bogged down trying to make decisions. They may tease, get angry, and then become provocative—but still cannot make a decision. Firm limit-setting helps a child like this not to get entangled in a web of mixed emotions, emotions which bring with them anxiety, despair, and even psychological paralysis.

LIMITS AND DISCIPLINE

We can talk about limits and discipline together, because although they do not completely overlap, they have teaching as their common goal: teaching a child rules of health and safety, making him pay attention to relevant aspects of his environment, helping him separate important from unimportant matters, and making it impossible for him to be successfully provocative. *Neither limits nor discipline should be used to punish in the sense of gaining revenge.*

Both "permissiveness" and "discipline" have been wildly misunderstood ideas.

Permissiveness was never meant to refer to actions, but only to feelings. Neither Sigmund Freud nor any other sensible psychologist, psychiatrist, or physician (including Benjamin Spock) ever felt a child should be allowed to *do* whatever he pleased. Instead, enlightened professionals said that rules and regulations should not be applied to a child's feelings, since the vast majority of feelings cannot be controlled without an extensive rethinking of personal values.

The purpose of discipline is not to hurt a child for something he has already done, but to make sure he does what is expected of him at the outset. The purpose of discipline is to channel a child in the right direction, not to hurt him, make him feel guilty, or blame him for his behavior.

Seeking to understand a child is not an alternative to discipline or limits. As we have noted, ardent advocates of corporal punishment seem always to make the false assumption that people live in a world of only two choices: one can be either a martinet who punishes or else a weakling on whom children and others walk. The disciples of the rod scream that we have ruined a generation of children by seeking to understand them. They somehow believe that anyone who seeks to understand a child *cannot at the same time limit and discipline him.* Why anyone should believe these patterns are mutually exclusive is hard to fathom. The alternative to not screaming, hitting, yelling, and cursing is not necessarily to be an indecisive individual who gives in on every important issue. Our system is very vigorous in insisting that children have very firm limits, and that there should be automatic follow-ups for noncooperation, but we are just as insistent that frequent physical punishment is futile in some cases and harmful in others.

We are not against physical discipline on moral grounds. But, as a general rule, physical punishment is both overused and useless. And even when the child confronts some danger, there are usually more effective ways to help him than by hurting him: removing him from the scene of the crime with a firm No will usually work.

As a matter of fact, the child on whom physical punishment works is usually the child on whom an explanation would have worked just as well. Some children respond very easily. One has only to say "Joan, if you don't behave, I'm going to force you . . ." and Joan rapidly behaves. With highly socialized children who cannot tolerate displeasing their parents, any kind of threat will work. Some parents assume that because something "works," it is right. Whips and branding irons, like hitting, would work in the short run. This hardly makes them right.

On the other hand, there is a whole range of children on whom physical discipline is not only ineffective but harmful. With such a child, physical discipline often either causes the child's problems to go underground, so that he modifies his surface behavior but inwardly learns nothing, or teaches the child that one solves problems by means of aggression—or just simply does not work. As we have seen, the child in need of negative attention will simply escalate the battle. The more we hit, the worse he gets. So we may win the individual battle, but we lose the war. He may behave for the moment but rarely will there be any staying power behind our physical assaults.

Spanking has been a major means of disciplining children for untold ages. If it is having any beneficial effects on humanity, it is hard to see them.

HOW TO SET LIMITS

Limits and discipline should respect the balance between the child's capabilities and that which is demanded of him, should be impersonal and easy to apply, and should have a channeling or funneling effect.

The very young child has to have his world limited to keep him safe, but it must also be structured so that it does not hopelessly confuse him by presenting him with an overabundance of stimulation. The playpen is an aid, as is not letting the child have unbridled freedom.

Limits are provided most gently for a young age by childproofing a house, so that you won't have to slap the child's hand every time he touches the bric-a-brac. By removing such articles and by reducing the amount of stimulation, you will introduce the child to a gentle yet firm set of limits as opposed to an overly harsh set of limits enforced by screaming.

Some parents object to childproofing and insist that a child should be taught not to touch pieces of bric-a-brac. This seems needlessly harsh to us. The exploratory urge of a child is intense and should be adequately satisfied. If you inhibit a child when he seeks to touch, feel, and explore his world, you may inhibit *all* curiosity and eventually his ability to learn.

On the other hand, a child may be taught he cannot touch things while in someone else's home. It is always permissible to teach appropriateness. There are many things a child may not be allowed to do in other homes that he is permitted to do in his own, such as taking off his shoes. There is nothing wrong with having a flexible set of standards as long as the child realizes there is a rational basis on which the rules are made.

If an object is dangerous to a child and yet cannot be removed from the child's reach—a television set, for example—your persistently removing the child from the object also constitutes fair, firm, and gentle limits. Carry the child away as many times as is necessary with a firm "No, you may not touch that." With the vast majority of children, this limit will be gradually accepted— if the parent shows a sense of conviction. Should the child sense weakness or indecision, he is less likely to accept the limit. And, again, if he is highly provocative, he may not accept the limit.

Physical discipline should be reserved for the rare instances in which the child's life is at stake, and a negative conditioning effect is desirable because the child cannot be removed from the danger. Most parents end up using physical discipline far too often because they are too nervous or too lazy to enforce some limit consistently. Yet in the long run things would be much simpler for them if they used limits instead of force.

Here is an example of what we mean by keeping rules and limits impersonal and easy to apply. In our house we have a rule that what-is-yours-is-yours. Suppose our oldest child owns a blackboard, which at the moment he is not using. Another child appears and asks to use it. The oldest refuses, and we feel he is just being "possessive": he really does not want to use the blackboard himself, but is determined his sibling shall not use it.

The typical parent would intervene. "You're being selfish. You're not using your blackboard. Why can't your brother have it?"

But to us this is not an effective way of handling the situation. We would support the decision of the oldest by repeating simply, "What's his is his." Contrary to what you may think, this kind of rule does not foster selfishness.

The rule is fair and consistent and makes it unnecessary for us to waste time trying to play judge and jury. It also makes sustained intervention unnecessary. And the importance of sharing can be developed in other contexts.

We put this same principle to work in another situation. We have a rule that when the noise level in the playroom reaches a certain intensity, the children must separate. This completely frees us from the hopeless task of trying to decide who did what to whom, and who is "guilty." It makes no difference who started the squabble or who is most at fault. When the noise level reaches a certain degree, separation follows.

Again, rules like this work well because they are fair and consistent. They prevent further argument.

The interesting thing is that we now have few arguments over who should play with what. Since there are clear-cut rules, and since no arguments can be sustained, the fun has gone out of this sort of neurotic dispute. No child bothers to protest should his brother or sister use one of his toys. Everyone knows no big deal will follow.

Now for an example of how to set up limits that are self-channeling. Many a parent complains that her child dawdles in the morning and will not take the responsibility of getting to school on time or of being ready for the school bus. You can say to such a child, "Look, you get up at seven-thirty now and are not ready to leave the house by eight-thirty unless we nag at you. Apparently one hour is not enough time for you. So we will help you get up half an hour earlier so you'll have more time. Of course, you will have to go to bed half an hour earlier, too. You can have as much time as you want. If you can't get ready in an hour and a half we will give you two hours, but of course you will go to bed that much earlier. You may end up going to bed in the middle of the afternoon, but we'll give you all the time you need."

In this way, the responsibility for the behavior is put where it belongs: in the lap of the child. Of course, everybody, including the child, knows that one hour is really enough time but that the child doesn't want the responsibility of getting himself ready. But the parent has a solution. If the child complains, "But I'll miss my favorite television program," he can be answered calmly, "We are not trying to punish you, but we want to help solve your problem. So however much time you need is what we'll give you."

A variation on this theme—a low-level, self-channeling system —is simply to tell a child he may not watch television until his homework is completed. Again the schedule can be set up so as to channel the child's behavior.

Much can be accomplished with young children if parents simply insist that limits be observed. Suppose your child has been told to clean the playroom, but doesn't do it. Instead of screaming and yelling and punishing him, it would be better for you to take him by the arm and say, "The playroom must be cleaned now. You have no choice." The child will see that you intend to enforce your limits with firm action—that there is an automatic follow-up to limits.

It is not always possible to use this approach, for a child is not always around to be led through missed activities. Suppose a teen-ager promises to come home at a certain time but does not. You cannot force him to come in if you do not know where he is, or if you do not want the job of tracking him down. So the answer may be simply to ground him for the next night. If he abuses his privilege again, he can then be grounded for two nights. It is important for him to see that how much freedom he gets rests squarely with him.

It is unwise to set harsh limits, because they lose their effectiveness. Often, in a fit of anger, a parent will scream that a child may not go out for a month. This can end as a punishment of the parent, for she has to endure having the child inside that long. It is far better to set limits in very small doses and gradually extend them if you need to.

We are not so naïve as to think that parents can be kept from ever getting angry, or that every instance of negative behavior on the part of the child can be handled in the manner we have suggested. But it is our belief that approximately 75 to 85 percent of difficult situations *can* be handled as outlined if the limits are set up and made clear in advance.

8
Foundation Skill 3:
Encouraging Independence

The term independence has broad, indefinite meanings today, but in this book it has a specific definition. By an independent child (or adult) we mean a person who is a self-starter, a self-sustainer, and a self-evaluator. An independent person is able to ignite his own spark and get himself moving; provide the fuel which sustains him through the completion of an endeavor; accept responsibility for evaluating his own performance. This last capability brings with it the power to withstand the negative and blaming opinions of others. As a result, the person is not defensive and so can appraise and accept relevant criticism.

THE IMPORTANCE OF INDEPENDENCE

Only a truly independent person is truly free and at the same time able to shoulder responsibility. Independence, freedom, and responsibility are overlapping capacities. Society will grant only that degree of freedom for which a man is willing to assume responsibility. Only those who are not devastated by the opinions

of others are able to operate without an intense fear of failure—
and hence can easily act responsibly.

Independence brings with it a true bonus as far as psychology
is concerned, for an independent person is one who does not
suffer from a crippling separation anxiety, the anxiety found at
the bottom of most neurotic conditions. Technically, separation
anxiety is a fear of losing the support and affection of an inner,
magical, omnipotent, maternal presence, but it may also be—
sometimes simultaneously!—a fear of smothering should the
presence draw too close. The child (or adult) fears he will die
should he separate, but if he moves too close he will annihilate
his autonomy as an individual. Since he intensely desires both
to be close and to be separate, he panics.

The independent child is able to separate from his parents.
At first this will be demonstrated by his ability to tolerate his
mother's absence. Later on, he will be able to sleep at friends'
homes. And gradually, he will be able to attend school and camp
without undue complaint.

The independent child does not nurture a secret, unconscious
longing for a complete union with his mother. This may not seem
important at a lay level, but psychologists realize that a person
with such an expectation is bound to demand endless maternal
satisfactions from his wife, whom he will expect to treat him as a
mother would a child. Such demands result in an almost impossible marital situation.

The independent child will neither demand constant attention nor be affected by a host of serious, neurotic conditions. And
he will show his better health in many everyday ways: he will
probably begin and complete his homework assignments without
prodding; he will more easily accept household chores; he will
have fewer nighttime fears; he will be less obnoxious and not
demand complete submission from those younger than himself.

DEVELOPING INDEPENDENCE

Part of the program to foster and develop independence is attitudinal: it depends on certain key attitudes or philosophies the parents should manifest toward the child.

The most important attitude you as parent must have—probably the decisive one—is the determination to view your child as a truly independent entity and not as some parental appendage, or as a means by which you are evaluated.

Here are some questions to ask yourself:

Are you overly concerned about what others, particularly your own parents, think of your child? Is your child to be your "champion"—your way of showing your own parents what a fine job you can do?

Do you confuse your fears with his? That is, do you unconsciously expect him to be afraid of the same things you are afraid of?

Does it hurt you deeply when the child does not adopt the exact values you would wish for him?

Are you easily upset when things do not go well for him? Do you find yourself stepping in to help instead of letting him muddle through on his own?

Father, if you were a poor fighter and inclined to be cowardly, is your son to be your revenge? Do you demand that he be the perfect fighter you were not? Do you become enraged at him when he fails to do well in a fight?

Mother, is your daughter to be perfect in all the things you do poorly?

Mother, are you using your children to show how giving you can be, how much you are able to sacrifice?

Are your main pleasures derived from your children's accomplishments?

Has your life settled into a routine where almost everything done is done for the children?

If your spouse is absent a good deal of the time, do you find yourself turning more and more to your child for companionship?

These are important issues. Go over this list of questions again, for it is easy to fool yourself. *Do you really see your child as a separate and distinct person?*

It is easy to confuse yourself on this issue of independence, for at the same time that you need to allow your children maximal freedom to muddle through on their own, you must also teach them many skills and must even demand conformity on many issues. So how do you draw the line?

Here we may speak of *parental intuition.* Intuition is the simultaneous appraisal of a complicated set of conditions, often too complex to spell out. In this context, the intuition refers to the parents' ability to gauge correctly the child's capacities at any given moment. Intuition is especially needed with a very young child who cannot put into words his desires and frustrations.

In order to grant independence you must be able to assess the balance between what a situation demands of a child and what the child's skills and capacities are. The balance determines the amount of independence that can be granted. Too many parents are overly worried and overly protective. If you are one of the overly fearful—overly involved about what others will think, and overly intent on having your child do everything perfectly—you will be unable to make balance judgments accurately. For the essence of the parental task is to allow the child to do what he is capable of doing *at the proper moment.* If timing is off, the child's willingness to pick up and do any activity on his own—to become a self-starter—will suffer. We are not saying that there is an exact moment when the child must be allowed to do a certain task on his own, but rather that there is a certain span of time when conditions are optimal: when the skill level and the interest level meet in a happy combination.

Here are some of the situations demanding parental intuition:

The time when your child is ready to feed and serve himself. Too many parents will not let a child pour his own milk into cereal because they are worried that he will make a mess.

The time for exploring. As we have suggested, a house should be "childproofed," so that a child is allowed the freedom to explore. You can still teach your child appropriate respect for property as he gets old enough to understand. But remember that a child whose exploratory drive is hampered is doomed to many future problems.

The readiness to dress himself. Some mothers simply do not want to take the time to allow a child to dress himself. But children who are dressed by their parents long past the age at which they would do so for themselves will soon not care to dress themselves at all and will turn the job over to their parents— permanently. This leads to a situation in which the mother yells at the child, "Why won't you dress yourself? Why are you always late in the morning? Why do you depend on me to dress you?" This mother may have saved herself a little bit of time in the beginning by dressing her child, but she pays dearly for it later.

The readiness to groom himself. Brushing the teeth, combing the hair, tucking in clothes, are all areas in which children can usually function independently long before their parents are willing to acknowledge.

You can judge whether you have both the psychological strength to allow your child's independence and the intuition to gauge when he can handle a task on his own by asking yourself whether you truly take joy in his functioning by himself—and whether you have the patience to allow him independent activity.

In fostering independence, you must learn to distinguish what can be *taught* from that which must be *learned*. There are many things in the world that cannot be taught, and these things you must have the patience to allow a child to learn. Getting dressed is an example. You can show a child several times how to put clothing on and how to button it. But if you watch, you will see that the child pays only indirect attention. He wants desperately to try for himself. Allow him to fumble around on his own until he masters the art. The ability to sit back and allow someone else to muddle through is one of the most basic and genuine hall-marks of the truly mature person.

Another thing that must be learned rather than taught is how to choose friends. Children often become infatuated with play-mates their parents consider undesirable. Many a parent will try to interfere and convince the child of the folly of his choice. The child then must defend his friend and so is unlikely to look at the weak spots in the friends' make-up. Instead of forcing your child into a defensive position, sit back and allow him to learn for him-self that he has made an unwise choice of a friend—unless you are dealing with a very young child who has chosen a dangerous friend or a teen-ager with a law-breaking friend: then parental action is justified.

In general, though, it is far better to allow the child to fumble around and learn things on his own than to step in and preach and teach. Too many parents have a need to drive a point home with every situation. Every single interaction becomes some sort of harangue with a moral. Children learn to tune out such "preachers."

If you have ever had an employer with the mature trait of patience, you know what a difference his attitude made in your job. *Secure in the knowledge that he would not rush in with advice, criticize you for your fumblings, or rob you of your initi-ative by taking over, you could pay greater attention to mastering the skill in question.*

People, including parents, seem to divide into two distinct categories—without a middle range. They tend either to be tolerant and patient and thereby excellent at engendering inde-pendence, or anxious, fussy, and inclined to step in too rapidly.

As we have noted, a crucial part of independence is self-evaluation. If you are to encourage your child to evaluate himself, you must teach him to be only appropriately concerned about the opinions of others. When he is not overly fearful of external opinions and confident of his own evaluations, he will become *more responsible for himself*. This is because the fear of making errors (a psychological force which prevents most people from

accomplishment) will be relatively reduced. Furthermore, *freedom from the blaming opinions of others is directly related to greater respect for the rights of others.*

A truly independent person is not a noncaring, cold individual. This is not what independence means. The independent person, sure of his own boundaries and self-confident, *is better able to love in a mature way* than is the dependent individual. The independent person's psychosocial motto might be: "I care very much what you think of me. I want you to love me as I love you. But I will not crumble and fall apart if you back away from me. I can afford to love you with all my heart because I do not worry about what will happen to me if you do not return my love. I am not afraid to show my love—anymore than I am afraid to lean on you and depend on you at times."

Here are some of the things you can do to encourage your child to be a self-evaluator:

1. When he shows you a piece of his work, good or poor, let him know that his opinions on its merits are more important than your own. This is *not* to say you should never praise or criticize, but it *is* to say you should tone down this aspect of your communications. Suppose a child shows you a rather good report card. Look at it and comment, "Fine—but what do *you* think about it since *that* actually is the important thing?" If he shows you a poor report card you might start out with a neutrally toned "I see" and then follow with the same "But what do you think about it? That is the important thing."

   You will find this approach not only teaches a child to evaluate things for himself but also encourages honesty and objectivity.

2. Teach the child to differentiate his feelings from his actions. Explain to him that limits are applied to *actions*, not to *feelings*. He is always free to feel any way he wants. Independence is *not* equivalent to license, but it *is* freedom from the negative evaluations of others.

   If a child beats up a younger sibling, you can stop him and

say, "You may not hit your brother." But you should not add anything about his feelings toward his brother, such as, "What are you doing? Brothers should love each other!"

3. Teach the child by your own example how to separate relevant criticism from blame. When you are criticized, learn to listen to the real kernel of the message. If it turns out you are doing something incorrectly, you can vow to improve things in the future. With long practice, you can learn to think, "Did I really make the mistake he is screaming at me for?" In some instances you may have to agree, "Yes, I think I did, and I will try not to make the same mistake again. But there is no need to blame myself for this mistake." Such thinking at first seems both stilted and dishonest—and it is, to some degree. But with time and hard challenging, you can make this your true attitude.

Remember that you should never tell yourself you are not upset if you really are. Acknowledge to yourself that you are furiously upset, should this be the case. But tell yourself also that this need not be so forever. And once you have mastered the principles, teach your child how to listen for the relevant aspects of criticism and how to ignore the blaming aspects.

4. Focus your child's attention on what he is doing rather than on how well he is doing it. Comment on the meaning of his project, not on his progress with it. He can do his own evaluating of his work—and his friends will do it for him anyway. So you can help balance the picture by seeing to it that he concerns himself with content and not with worry over his skill.

THE CHILD WHO HAS NOT BECOME INDEPENDENT

There are two strategies to use with such a child, but they must both be used. One aims to confront him with the fact that he is not appropriately independent, and the other aims to channel him in an independent direction.

The first strategy is accomplished through the use of so-called weaning interpretations by which the child—without feeling crushed—may be made to recognize his dependent behavior and to realize that he would feel much better were he more independent.

Weaning interpretations come in two stages. The first stage aims simply to show the child what he is doing:

"Johnny, you have gotten to the point where you do not do your homework unless we push, yell, and force you. But we don't want the job of prodding you. So we hope you will pick up the ball on your own."

"Simon, it seems as though there are a good many things you won't do unless we yell. But we're not interested in yelling."

In this stage, your only aim is to confront the child with the fact that he rarely acts unless forced. You must make your statements in a nonblaming, calm way. If you do not, your child will not listen. (If you cannot point out your child's behavior in a calm tone of voice, postpone the conversation until you can.) Even under the best of conditions, the child will not really pay attention to what you are saying the first couple of times. But, if you persist—without blame or anger—eventually he will stop and ask himself the magic question: "Is that really what I'm doing?"

Once he asks himself this question, he has taken twenty giant steps forward: he has attempted to adopt someone else's point of view. And once he has shown himself capable of tolerating interpretations of his behavior, he is ready for the second stage.

The second stage of weaning interpretations aims to make the child realize what he has hoped to accomplish by his dependent behavior: to maintain the identity status role of child. This more advanced interpretation might be expressed as follows:

"Johnny, you have gotten to the point where you do not do things unless you are pushed. Now there is a part of all of us that does not want to grow up—that wants to remain childlike. Sometimes this part of our personality can get so strong that it takes over the rest and tries to get adults to boss it around.

"You may not realize it, but when you do not do things for yourself that you should be doing, it is not simply because you are lazy but because you actually *want us* to treat you like a child. That part of you finding it tough to grow up wants to be treated like a baby—and gets to be by forcing *us* to force you."

This type of interpretation shows the child the unconscious dependency urges behind his nonresponsible behavior, his babyish demand that others care for him.

As the weaning interpretations come to be accepted (this may take anywhere from one day to two months—and longer in extreme cases), gradually begin steering the child toward independence by making use of his own natural desires. One such low-level self-steering system is that the child cannot watch television until he has completed his homework. Another is that the child cannot go outside until his playroom is picked up. In each case, the child's desire to accomplish some goal will push him to do the nondesired things.

Too many parents begin to use these systems but abandon them because they are unwilling to expend the energy it requires to force the child to comply in the initial stages. And it takes energy. A child who does a slipshod job on the playroom should be sent back as many times as are required for him to do a better job.

Other low-level self-propelling systems should be set up so that the dependent child gets privileges equal only to that which he has shown himself capable of handling. Suppose a teen-ager asks how many nights out he may have. He can be told he may have as many as he shows himself capable of handling. As long as he takes care of his health, schoolwork, and household chores, the rest of his time is his own. Choose an arbitrary number of nights out per week as the starting point. If he shows himself able to handle his obligations, add more nights—until some limit or balance is reached. This child can in all honesty be told, "You may have as much freedom as you can handle. You may end up with being able to go out six or even seven nights. You may also end up going out no nights. It depends completely on you." The system helps to guide his own behavior.

If, however, a child has shown himself absolutely unable to guide his own behavior a more elaborate procedure may have to be worked out. The child must be asked to agree beforehand both to the chores and to the limits or "follow-ups" to be used if he does not honor his *own* agreements.

Suppose, for example, it is determined that the child is not doing his homework, although he could do it. The night wears on and nothing happens. The parents get more upset and would like to step in, in their usual way, "Damn it, Ralph. Do your homework!" But instead they first introduce a stage-one weaning interpretation: "Ralph, you don't do your homework unless we yell at you and we make you do it. But we don't want the job. We don't like to yell at you. We hope you do it on your own."

This should be tried three or four times and if Ralph's inhibitions are stronger, the stage-two interpretation should be made: " . . . and the part of you that wants to remain a child has chosen "homework" as the battlefield. This is the area in which you want us to know you don't want to grow up—that you would rather we treat you like a baby by *making* you do it."

If further action is needed, homework should be discussed at a family meeting. Each person should give his version of the purposes of homework and *each* child should be allowed to set up his own system for doing it, including Ralph. If Ralph does not observe his *own* system, he can be told, "Ralph, this system is not working even though you designed it yourself. We must ask you to design another." The parents may agree to a limited role as reminders and gradually phase themselves out via weaning interpretations.

You will notice that this program is a channeling one. The parent does not completely force the child into doing the work for himself, nor does he completely back away. A child used to being carried along by his parents may collapse if total support is withdrawn immediately. Yet if the parent continues to carry the child who can walk but won't, the child's independence is just pushed further and further into the future. As long as a child who can walk is carried, he will never walk on his own.

A step somewhere in between complete domination on the one hand and complete withdrawal is needed. We feel a system that combines weaning interpretations with self-steering strategies furnishes the middle ground.

9

Foundation Skill 4: Acknowledgments; Encouraging Self-induced Change

There are two basic types of acknowledgments. One is a simple reflection of a condition: "Johnny, it is very difficult for you to resist teasing your brother." The other is a simple *genuine* acceptance of a feeling: "You are quite upset and angry now."

Both types of acknowledgments, if delivered in a genuinely accepting tone of voice and without preaching, can help a youngster or adult confront some aspect of his own behavior and eventually deal more effectively with it.

There are a number of purposes served by acknowledgments:

1. They help a child to recognize his negative behavior patterns or the absence of a positive pattern.
2. They foster independence by implicitly showing a child he is trusted to play a large part in changing and guiding his own behavior.
3. They provide the child with a nonsmothering type of en-

couragement. He feels less isolated because someone else knows how he feels.

4. They help the child mobilize his own resources to deal with his problems. He is encouraged by the nonblaming, non-manipulative approach to confront his problems and solve them for himself, and by the hand-on-the-shoulder attitude to feel that someone is standing behind him—someone who cares.

HELPING THE CHILD RECOGNIZE
HIS OWN DIFFICULTIES

As we saw in our discussion of weaning interpretations (Chapter 8), the next to hardest step to take in changing behavior is to recognize that the behavior in fact exists. (The hardest step is to agree inwardly that the behavior should in fact be changed.) Actually, often mere recognition of the behavior is an implicit admission that it would be better to change it.

Children are exceedingly resistant to recognizing that they do indeed engage in negative behavior patterns. It is as if they know that behavior change would be just around the corner. Often the behavior in question is so obnoxious that the child just *cannot* admit to it, so harsh would be his judgment of himself if he did.

Acknowledgments aim to bring recognition of the difficulty and to provide the "distance" by means of which the child can agree the behavior should perhaps be changed.

Because you are *not blaming* the child for his behavior but merely reflecting or acknowledging it, because you are not robbing the child of his own initiative by asserting you are better able to solve his problems than he is, and because you are showing the child that you do indeed care, you are offering him an opportunity to recognize, confront, and see his own behavior more objectively. Since yours is a nonblaming attitude, the child feels relatively less inclined to defend his negative position. *He can look at it because he does not have to make excuses for it. He can even consider changing it, because to do so will not be an admission of defeat.* If a person is not attacked for occupying a territory, he will feel no disgrace in abandoning it.

Compare these two approaches:

"My God, Johnny, you never do your homework!"

"Johnny, it seems that you do not do your homework unless we yell at you."

The first is an accusation; the second is a simple acknowledgment or reflection of a state of affairs. The first calls for a defense: "I do so do my homework. What do you mean I don't do my homework. I always do my homework!"

When a child has a reality condition acknowledged, he is not even called upon to respond out loud. He can rather eventually say to himself, "That's true—I really don't do my homework unless someone forces me." In short, since an acknowledgment requires no defense, it provides the child with a psychological breathing space, an opportunity to step back and look at his own behavior.

But please note that an acknowledgment does not always get immediate results. Its purpose is to allow the child to see, confront, and change his behavior *eventually*. The child will likely ignore acknowledgments the first number of times, even though he hears them. Eventually, though, the neutrally toned statements will allow the child to ask himself what we call the "golden words": "Why *do* I do that?" When a child finally brings himself to ask if or why he really does something, he is in a position *to do something* about the negative behavior.

It is far better to wait, however long it takes, for the child to ask himself the golden words than it is to scream accusations at the child—who then will never ask himself these questions at all. Nor does it help to use simple rewards like candy, which often accomplish nothing in the long run. Acknowledgments speak with soft tones, but are eventually heard.

LETTING THE CHILD KNOW
HE DOES NOT STAND ALONE

There are a number of bad situations in which there is really nothing much parents can say: for example, when a child has been hurt, embarrassed, or beaten up by a peer. And yet most parents find all kinds of wrong or nonhelpful things to say under these circumstances.

Suppose the child is in a fight. He backs down or loses and is bruised in the process. He comes home crying. The typical father is annoyed (unconsciously enraged) that his son has lost the fight. He may yell, "Well, that's what happens when you can't defend yourself!" Or he may insist that the child go back out and do a better job.

It would be far smarter simply to acknowledge the child's hurt: "It's very upsetting and painful to lose a fight." This homely little remark is exceedingly helpful from a psychological standpoint. It lets the child know his parent understands exactly how he feels. *The child feels accepted in spite of the fact that he lost the fight.* This is tremendously important. People can build more efficient personalities on foundations of love and acceptance than on blame. It is hard if not impossible to build a positive personality with anger, disgust, and criticism.

When a child feels he is not being condemned for some bit of behavior, he can afford to move ahead in a constructive way. He can vow to do better next time. His self-confidence is enhanced by the acknowledgment of hurt feelings, instead of being pounded by further rejecting criticism.

Many parents think that an acknowledgment may encourage tearful complaining. This is to confuse excessive sympathy with an acknowledgment. The latter is a simple, matter-of-fact, but genuine indication of understanding and acceptance. It does not encourage griping; by contributing to a better and stronger self-image, it decreases the chance of griping.

A shy or unassertive or pathologically unaggressive child is one who feels so isolated and blamed for his inefficient past behavior that he cannot mobilize his own resources. When the father simply places a hand on his child's shoulder and shows that he knows how his son feels, the boy is encouraged to act constructively.

There are a number of other situations in which the only sensible behavior on the part of the parent is to make a simple acknowledgment of feeling:

"Why can't I go with you? You never take me!"

"My brother always gets better marks than I do! It's not fair!"

"The other kids won't play with me!"

In all of these instances, the most helpful parent will look at the child, think of what the child is going through, and respond with, "That must be a rotten feeling" or "I can really understand how you feel."

But it is extremely important that the parents think about how the child is feeling before they make an acknowledgment. It must be an honest process. The mere parroting of words will have no effect or possibly even a negative effect.

The acknowledgment of feelings does not aim to accomplish a great deal in the immediate situation. It is hardly going to transform the child who has just been beaten in a fight, or the child who feels frustrated because of some real or imagined injustice, or the one who feels his brother gets better school marks (especially if he *does*). Yet the acknowledgment is a thread in a fabric. Although the immediate problem is not solved at once, the child's overall resources are strengthened and the goal becomes a potential reality.

SERIOUS MISBEHAVIOR

Sometimes a situation demands that an acknowledgment be combined with more definite action.

One of the most effective ways to help a noncooperative child cope eventually with a responsibility is simply to walk him through it—use a very low-level, nonaggressive, physical insistence accompanied by a direct acknowledgment: "I know you're very hurt and upset, but this is something you have to do."

When the child's behavior must be stopped immediately because it is dangerous or obnoxious, or because there isn't time to wait for the child to change it on his own—for example, when he is hurting a younger sibling—proceed with the simple setting of limits, and use the acknowledgment as an adjunct.

10

The Family Council

The family council may be described as a limited democracy (or a benign dictatorship) in which goals, responsibilities, and limits are set and debated by all members of the family but the ultimate authority rests with the parents.

Since parents bear the majority of responsibility for the health and safety of the family, its economic planning and management, and the lion's share of the burden of its setbacks and misfortunes, the council cannot be based on a one man, one vote system. Authority in a decision-making system must be proportional to responsibility for consequences. And though some matters, such as health and safety rules, are not open to much debate, there *is* wide area for compromise and plenty of room for discussion. The council meetings should be held weekly at first, and later as often as the family requires.

Everyone should be invited. (Even three- and four-year-olds will be interested if the meetings start with the issues relevant to them, and if they are excused immediately afterward, so that their participation is brief and lively.) Though everyone in the family is welcome, no one must be forced to attend meetings. But *everyone living under the parental roof must abide by the decisions of the council.*

The idea of a regularly held, formally run meeting is certainly not new, but in our opinion nothing resembling its potential advantages has been realized. There are great psychological advantages to having children and adults make prior commitments. When a child carries out a chore he himself agreed to do in advance, he is not submitting to pressure, and he suffers no loss of pride or status.

A council system gives families a continuing way to implement their decisions. Many families are good at coming up with plans but poor at carrying them out.

And the family council makes it easier to deal with unpleasant aspects of interaction by providing a formal structure, for all of the gripes and complaints are handled at one time instead of being spread over an entire week. Furthermore, the formality of the meeting provides the kind of protection or "psychological distance" a resistant teen-ager needs if he is to chance close interaction with his family; the child with leftover dependency needs may mock the formality, but it will be his ally in dealing with his parents.

A family council arrangement may be more necessary today than in earlier times because the forces operating on the contemporary family—the impact of mass media; the sanctioning of rebellion against authority—change the options open to modern parents. Young people are in touch with each other today via mass media, including underground newspapers. They know that others of their age are rebelling all over the world. The problems in setting effective limits for them are vastly different from those which faced parents in bygone eras when teen-agers were not united. And yet with youth at a loss to know what values to embrace and with many adults just as confused, there is currently no existing medium of communication *between* the generations. The family council will not solve the communication gap, but it will be a help.

For the children, a major psychological "plus" of the council is that no rule or agreement need be considered permanent. All rules can be rediscussed, but *no agreed-upon responsibilities can be dropped between councils.* This arrangement allows the parents to tell a noncooperative child, "This is what you agreed to do at the council [or what the council assigned you]. If you feel it's unfair, bring it up at the next council. But for now, you must do it."

Children rarely mind accepting limits and responsibilities once they are assured of a continuing court of appeals. Actually, it is the *assurance* of this privilege that children seek; once they have it, they seldom exercise it.

Fundamentally, every child wants a strong family. The idea of a cohesive family structure is intensely appealing. And so the family council has proven popular even with very disturbed children who seemed to have no great love for fellow family members. (Only when the council is used as a gimmick to control or manipulate one particular child—a disastrous mistake—does it fail.)

The council will even help unify siblings who were previously at each other's throats, for they will discover the advantages of cooperation. They will present "interlocking pieces of legislation" since they will have mutual concerns. Although their unity will not always hold, it will have a good chance to develop.

The council system serves to break up neurotic two-person battles, by turning them into issues involving the entire family. After all, the source of most of the rules and regulations is the entire family group. The council prevents the kind of situation in which a daughter fights her mother because the daughter feels that the mother makes all the decisions. Then, too, since the rules are set up in advance, the children know that they do not emanate from arbitrary whims. (When rules vary in accordance with parental moods, then a child rightly feels it makes sense to needle or assault the parent to get them changed again.)

A family council shows the children *both* parents truly care about what is going on and makes it difficult to play one parent against the other, for everything is out in the open. As we know, children are notorious at playing parents against each other.

The council gives the children a chance to observe their father in a truly masculine role, that of effective decision-maker and settler of disputes. And it can have a profoundly positive effect on the relationship between husband and wife since it more or less insures that the husband will have a continuing interest in running the family efficiently, without conflict. When a woman sees that she does not stand alone, she will feel more favorably disposed toward her husband.

Too many fathers confine their leadership abilities to their jobs and are "tired ploppers" at home. They show no continuing interest in their growing children. Once every few weeks they yell at everybody, and take this as evidence of paternal interest. The family council optimizes the chances of the father's making a much more genuine commitment to the family, for it fosters a very explicit pulling together periodically—without demanding a never-ending, smothering "togetherness."

THE FATHER AS GROUP LEADER

If a family has both a mother and a father, the council should be headed by the father. If, on the other hand, there is no father, the mother can head the council just as she heads the family. It is an altogether different situation when a family lacks a father because there isn't any from when there is a father and he refuses the role. A single-parent family can survive and flourish though the road is not an easy one. A family in which the father has abdicated is another matter, for here we deal with a possible sexual imbalance, distorted decision-making patterns, and mutual sabotage.

In a two-parent family, the most decisive element in determining the success of the family council will be the father's ability to be an effective group leader. He must overcome any initial uneasiness he feels because of the semiformality of the procedure, for if he departs from it, he will find the children gradually lose their respect for the councils. As we noted, they may mock the formality at first ("Jeez, is that square"), but they are unconsciously attracted to the protection it affords, and their support will gradually emerge.

The father must deflect any attempts at disruption. Should a child giggle, he might say, "I can understand how you feel. We often cover our anxiety by laughing." In this way the child has had his laughing accepted for what it is, a manifestation of anxiety over what he may be letting himself in for. And the father has prevented the laughing from disrupting the council. If a teen-ager says, "This is stupid," the father could answer, "I can see where you might feel that way, but we'd like to try it anyhow. Let's see how it works out." The aggression is not shoved back down the boy's throat, and the teen-ager is not forced into a position where he must defend himself, because the father does not counter the hostility with his own. Gradually, the boy will be intrigued enough to join in—and will probably do a lot of the talking.

A severely disruptive child can be reminded he need not join in the council meetings if he does not want to, and that he can rejoin the group whenever he decides to. Telling such a child that he can leave but rejoin the group any time he wishes saves face for the father, for the hostile one, and the council. Since the child is neither blamed nor mocked, he does not feel forced to remain out of the group to support his initial defiance. And yet since he is "removed," the father has not lost control of the council by allowing it to be disrupted. Should the children discover that their father blows up if they act silly or defiant, they will find themselves in possession of a means of wrecking any meeting not going their way. By remaining calm, the parent stays firmly in command.

The father should review to himself all he knows about being a good group leader. It is important that he makes sure everyone gets a fair hearing, and that the council does not begin to resemble a Star Chamber.

SOME SUGGESTED STRATEGIES

1. Start the first meeting by discussing a number of points: that a family cannot run smoothly unless everyone cooperates; that even though parents have final authority, there is plenty of room for debate; that the family council is not going to be a place just to make rules and to lodge complaints but also to discuss ways of having fun; that all gripes will be given a fair hearing.

   The father might explain about dividing responsibilities. "Society got started when one man approached another and said, 'You hunt better than I do and I build houses better than you do. If you do the hunting for us both, I will build houses for us both.' In this way people learned that by co-operating they could do better. Mutual cooperation is still the basis of society." Children will realize the basic honesty of this explanation, however corny they think it.

   The father might then ask, "Do parents owe their children anything?" All of the children will agree they do. "Do children owe their parents anything?" Most children will agree they do. This would be the time to discuss chores, the dividing up of responsibilities for running the family. Remember to discuss at least one pleasant thing (vacation plans, weekend plans) at the first meeting.

   And let the children bargain something to their own advantage at the first meeting. It is helpful if they see the council as something that will work for them—as much if not more than against them.

2. Caucus with your mate ahead of time on crucial points—but don't carry this idea to an extreme. In fact, it is a grave mistake for parents to vote a straight party line—Mom always for Dad, Dad for Mom. More important than the caucus itself will be the *attitudes* husband and wife manifest toward each other. Does he undermine her by laughing at her ideas? Does

she sabotage his influence by carrying on side conversations while he is talking? Nowhere will a lack of unity at the top of the structure show so blatantly as at a council. Yet nowhere will the positive effects of good parental unity work to such advantage. Remember that the children's awareness of parental unity strengthens them over the long haul, even though they sometimes resent it.

3. Keep rules and regulations as few as possible, and as simple as possible. One of the parents should keep the minutes. A simple rule is one like "When the noise level gets too high, everyone separates." A complicated rule might, under the same circumstance, involve a long procedure for trying to establish differential guilt and penalties.

Explain to the children how certain rules are more important than others and must be obeyed immediately. A wastebasket that is frequently used must be emptied as soon as it is filled. A child who has this chore should realize it must be carried out immediately. He can be shown that other chores—cleaning his room, emptying little-used baskets—can be done at a more leisurely pace.

Remember that when children realize your decisions are not arbitrary, they are likely to cooperate. Too many parents foul themselves up by being needlessly arbitrary and by acting as though a "low-level" rule has the same degree of urgency as a "high-level" one. They justify themselves by saying their parents did the same to them!

When parents act inconsistently or arbitrarily, children tune them out. This does not mean children should have every rule explained to them before they follow it. A child should be informed that there are instances, particularly in situations involving health and safety, when he may ask no questions at all but must act immediately. A child can generally tell from the tone of your voice the type of situation he is dealing with.

4. Come up with automatic follow-ups for situations in which a child does not carry out his agreements. Remind him first of his pledge: "This is something you already agreed to do." If a

young child does not carry out what he has agreed to do, walk him through the activity.

Let the child vote on his own follow-up. For example, let the child who agrees to spend a certain amount of time on homework agree also on what limit he must accept should he not do the homework: for example, no television until he carries out his own agreement.

When you find yourself having to remind a child of something an endless number of times, bring the dilemma up at a council meeting. Say to the child, "I am willing to remind you *sometimes*, but not all the time. How many times should I remind you to carry out the chore, before I proceed with the limits?" Let the child determine how many times he is to be reminded. There is nothing wrong with a parent reminding a child to do something *provided it has been discussed in advance.*

It is one thing for a parent to have to nag a child through the day; it is quite another thing when there is a formal agreement to give reminders. In the former case, the child is blackmailing the parents into being responsible for him. In the latter case, the child has helped set up the system himself.

5. Discuss all punishments and limits at the council. You will find children have a tendency to be far more ruthless with themselves than their parents are. Don't let this be carried to extremes. If one child tries to impose an overly harsh punishment on a sibling, channel him into exercising constraint.

6. Extend as much freedom as is consistent with the child's ability to handle things. We are referring to privileges such as the number of nights out, the number of hobbies, etc. There is no reason why a child should not be given the *upper limits of freedom he has proven himself capable of handling.* As we have said, if your older child asks how many nights out he may have, you might answer: "As many as you can handle—from one to seven. Your responsibilities involve homework, chores, and your personal health. Our only concern is that you do what you have agreed to do and take care of your health."

Telling him he can have as much freedom as he can handle gives him something to aim for and places responsibility for his freedom on his own shoulders. Should he argue that you are not giving him enough freedom you can answer, "You are the one who determines how much freedom you get. The more you handle your responsibilities, the more freedom you will earn."

7. If a child has a long history of being uncooperative, make sure he gets his new chores one at a time over a substantial length of time (perhaps three months). In this way, he will not feel overwhelmed. It is always better to have a few rules enforced than many rules poorly applied.

Young children have a tendency to agree to too many rather than to too few chores—and then later to refuse them, thereby weakening the system. Handle such a situation by saying, "You may do the additional things if you want, but we won't expect them and we won't write them in the minutes." In this way, the authority of the council is not threatened.

8. Be prepared to deal with the situations that need special handling. Should a child make a ridiculous demand—say a seven-year-old demand to go to bed at 1 A.M.—his father might say, "When you make impossible demands you are really trying to tell me you do not want to bargain. You would rather I tell *you* when to go to bed. If you make demands which are impossible to bargain with, that is just what will happen." This is no gimmick. If someone comes to a bargaining table in bad faith to make impossible demands, compromise is impossible. So when children make impossible demands, the parents must assume full control. But the child should be told that when he is reasonable it will be possible to bargain with him again.

A child who hogs the meeting can be told, "Jimmy, you seem to want us to pay exclusive attention to you. OK—you may have the first ten minutes all to yourself, then you may leave, even though this will mean that you will miss talking about some of the fun things."

Again, if the child is openly aggressive he can be told, "Johnny, you are trying to tell us you do not want to attend the meeting. Fine. You do not have to. You will *still* have to abide by all the rules that come out of the meeting, but you just won't have a say in them. You may leave now, but you may rejoin us any time you feel in control of yourself. You may decide to come back right now or in five minutes or in a half hour or maybe not until the next meeting. Whenever you want to, the door will be open."

A child may say he does not want to attend at all—that he is not interested in a family council. He can be told, "You do not have to attend. The only penalty for not attending is that you won't have a voice in the decisions. But aside from that there are no hard feelings on either side, although we'd rather you'd join us. The decision is completely yours."

Remember that the children will assign the same importance to the family council as you, the parents, do. If you constantly interrupt the procedure—leave to answer the phone, become overly distracted—so too will the children. If you assign it importance, so will the children.

Typically, by the fifth or sixth meeting you will find you have covered most of the important sources of difficulty in the running of the house. When this point is reached, even though the family council may still be an enjoyable affair, interest in it may diminish somewhat. The children will probably still like it, though the father may find himself not interested in running the meetings any longer because everything is going smoothly. This will be too bad, for his disinterest will sap the council of later potential usefulness.

It would be better to conclude one of the meetings by saying: "Things seem to be working smoothly. Why don't we call our next meeting for about three or four weeks from now. If however, anything comes up, anyone may feel free to call a meeting." By setting wider intervals between meetings, the council will not run out of steam, but will remain an important aspect of family interaction.

IF THE FATHER REFUSES TO PRESIDE

We have stressed the importance of having the father be the group leader, and yet there are fathers who refuse to cooperate with their wives or to take the need for such help seriously. Their excuses are many:

"I'm busy with work."

"A father's job is to make money; the mother should raise the kids."

"I never see the kids anyway."

"I'm never around when the kids do bad things."

"The kids always obey me; it's you they won't listen to."

Such a father may give lip service to the idea that things are not right, but he isn't interested in trying out a new or different approach. It is crucial that he be made to realize that no system can work without his active support; that the amount of time he spends with his children is less important than the *quality* of time spent; and, most important, that for any family to have effective organization, each member must feel the father's willpower and his determination that things be organized.

In the case of a husband's noncooperation, his wife should pay special attention to the procedure for communicating without blame and should also do her best to have her mate read Part I of this book. When both husband and wife realize the negative forces that may have been active throughout their marriage, underlying hostility may subside. But the book has to be presented unemotionally to the noncooperative mate: "I would like to have your help in trying to understand what's going on around here," and *not* "It's your fault things are messed up, so why don't *you* read this book and see what *you've* been doing wrong." It is exceedingly unlikely that any parent ever deliberately set out to hurt a child, so the concept of blame is truly out of place in a helping program.

If the noncooperation is more extreme—if communication with

a mate is really strained—some neutral third party—a bright friend, a trusted clergyman—should be asked to help convey the importance of trying to forge a more effective family.

And if the husband will neither cooperate nor seek personal help—a great many men consider the need for help a sign of weakness—it may prove beneficial for the wife to seek professional consultation. It is often possible for a psychotherapist to assist the cooperative parent to reach the spouse. (It is not unusual for the ultimate picture to look quite different from the early one—for example, the initially uncooperative mate may turn out to be the healthier of the two.)

TO SUM UP

You will find that decisions made in front of a family group have a staying power not equaled by decisions made between two people, and that children are much better at carrying out commitments on which they have made prior agreements. You will find also that neurotic interaction between family members is reduced, and that you and your mate pull together more of the time. You will find a new form of cohesiveness in the family and that even rebellious teen-agers, who at first mocked the council idea, are now leading contributors to it.

The previously resistant child will find himself confronted with a nonblaming but united structure. Psychologically, it is very easy for a misbehaving child to ignore a nagging mother standing alone; it is quite another thing to disregard a unified, nonviolent, but exceedingly firm family structure.

But all these results will not be obtained quickly. It will take a number of weeks to get the system to function smoothly. Do not be upset if the opening meeting does not proceed well. Do not try to accomplish more than one really important or serious point at any single meeting. Have patience. Keep in mind also that the family council is being used as part of an overall system.

Each part of the system will reinforce other parts. The foundation skills will make it much easier to use the family council, while the council will assist greatly in applying the foundation skills.

11

Special Strategies for the Out-of-Control Child

There are many reasons why a child may have poor self-control. He may suffer from a desire to punish himself and his parents. He may have some biological difficulty (a glandular abnormality, mild or severe brain damage). He may suffer from a disability in which he is subjected to intense bursts of psychoneurological energy, e.g., epilepsy. Some instances of aggressive, uncontrolled behavior result from a failure to develop a proper set of civilized attitudes, as in the case of a psychopath, whose hostility is not mitigated by concern for his victim's fate.

With the exception of the psychopath, the great majority of uncontrolled people come to have two traits in common: provocativeness, a gradually developed need to incite negative emotions in others; and demandingness, a stronger than usual desire to control others, no matter what confrontations are necessary. Sometimes these traits seem to develop as part of another problem, as with the overly manipulated child who yearns for complete "fusion" with his version of an all-giving, omnipotent mother. In other cases the need for negative attention and the demands seem to form in reaction either to a physical disability or to faulty parental handling, as with the mother who is unable to deal with the normal-for-the-condition insatiable needs of the child with mild brain damage. Children with brain damage often attempt to gain an intact self-image and/or greater self-esteem by making endless demands on their parents; the parents must remain sympathetic to the child *while at the same time setting proper limits*, or the child's appetite will mount in ever-increasing cycles.

All out-of-control children come to seek negative attention one way or another. This has already been explained in detail (in Chapter 7) as an attempt to reduce the increased separation anxiety by blackmailing the parents into furnishing the child with intense negative, highly personal, emotions. The child, as it were, seeks to invade and take over his parent's awareness.

In all families with uncontrolled children, provocativeness and demandingness, and their results, gradually dominate the day-by-day confrontations and difficulties. And so the treatment program outlined here is designed to reduce these traits.

The prime strategy for dealing with a provocative, demanding, uncontrolled child is for the parents to set up a situation in which they will receive enough psychological protection to remain extremely sympathetic and nonblaming toward the child, *while at the same time* setting appropriate limits. All the love and permissiveness in the world will not cure or even "dent" the provocative, out-of-control child. But, on the other hand, you can punish such a child day and night and nothing will happen.

Two conditions seem necessary:

1. A proper setting of limits by which the child is shown he can survive and flourish without negative emotion, limits that prevent him from becoming overwhelmed by the intensity of his own needs. Although he may balk at the limits, he is unconsciously grateful for them, for he realizes deep down that they guarantee his own and your survival.
2. Your continued warm, nonblaming sympathy increases his

motivation to shake off negative emotions and reduces his basic separation anxiety, by showing him that even when he goes out of control he will not lose his parents as allies.

All children need nonblaming warmth and firm limits. Out-of-control children need them especially. So, as a matter of fact, do the rebellious ones of today.

All of the strategies in this book—the council, reducing blame, and so forth—collectively aim to help the parents achieve these ideals. The council provides a semiformal system for dealing concretely with out-of-control children. Not only does the council help set limits on the children's insatiable needs, but it *affords a measure of protection to the parents* who can then muster some of their prior warmth for their often obnoxious children.

Before going on to additional measures which may be used with extreme cases, we want to discuss a most important aid in setting limits, the so-called "quiet" or "time-out" room. It is useful with all children occasionally, but with highly uncontrolled ones frequently.

THE TIME-OUT ROOM

The room may appear under many labels: the time-out room because the child is removed so to speak from "normal" time and activities; the quiet room because it is a quiet sanctuary in which it is hoped the child will regain control; the out-of-bounds room because the child's behavior was out of the range of the acceptable. It is never to be called a "punishment" or "penalty" room because this is not its purpose. True, a child sent there may feel punished. But the purpose of the room is to give him a chance to regain self-control. Since he is not there to be punished, he can rejoin normal activities as soon as he is in control.

A child should be sent there only as a last resort.

In a school, this room should be easily accessible from the classroom, and should be constructed to allow the teacher to see in, but so that the pupil cannot see out. It should have a lock on the outside, but this should be used only if necessary, and in conjunction with caution (the risk of forgetting the child in an emergency, etc.).

At home, since rooms are scarce, the child's bedroom can be used as the time-out room even if he has many toys and games there. Since the purpose is *not* to punish him, it does not matter whether he plays and otherwise has a good time. He will have been removed from the situation in which he could not control himself.

The room has many purposes: to help the child gain self-control by reducing the amount of stimulation to which he is exposed (this is the main purpose); to stop negative patterns from spreading out over the entire household or class; to disrupt negative behavior that is building to a dangerous and excessive level (some children are terrified by a fear that their emotions will build to a level at which they will be totally out of control); to prevent the reinforcement by repetition of negative behavior patterns; to disrupt patterns and interchanges that are sure to become neurotic between parent or teacher and child if allowed to continue.

Hence, a multiplicity of purposes intermesh in the operation of the room. They are not all therapeutic, or not therapeutic to the same degree. In school, a child may be placed there simply because not to so place him would disrupt the entire class. Or a child may be sent there to lessen the stimulation to which he is exposed, and hence serve to relieve the burden on an already strained self-control mechanism. Another child may be there for both purposes.

Since certain children will view the room as a punishment regardless of what you say or do, some aspects of the room will have ambiguous meaning and significance. There is no way around this. You may pay the price of allowing the child to feel punished in order to buttress his self-control and allow your household or class to continue. One is often not sure how to draw up the balance sheet, and at what point one may be paying too high a price for a gain. To specify the exact degree of disorganization a household or class should tolerate before the disorganizing child is excluded would involve a hopelessly complex set of decision rules. One would have to consider the nature of the other children present, the degree of "strain" these others can tolerate, the balance, or health, of the currently disruptive child, the parent's or teacher's strength, and so forth. In other words, there will always be a good bit of educated guessing in using a time-out room.

Here are some suggestions on the use of a time-out room.

A child should be sent to it for brief periods only and no more than one child should occupy it at a given time. About two minutes before he is to come out, knock on the door to prepare him. If he is still not in control of himself, extend the time. Very often, the child himself can decide when to come out. This is especially true of a child who has identified with the parent or teacher to some extent, and who voluntarily commits himself to the time-out room when he feels a loss of control coming on. If the plan is to allow the child to choose the time of his exit, but he persistently comes out before he is ready, the parent or teacher will have to set some arbitrary time.

Should a child leave the room you may have to walk him back to it. Even if you have to do so a number of times, maintain a calm, matter-of-fact manner. Should this fail, and should you not wish to use a lock, you may have to deal with the child in some other way. In a school, he may be sent to the principal's office or to a "roving teacher" or to a resident psychotherapist who can interpret the negative behavior; at home it may be wiser simply to avoid any confrontation until his father is home.

But the room itself should not become a neurotic battleground. A child should not be sent there by a screaming parent since this would reinforce his difficulties. The rules for its use should be clearly understood. A child should be sent there matter-of-factly: "The rule here is that when someone does so-and-so, he has to go in the time-out room and try to gain some control."

It is not always easy to decide when to use the room. It has its liabilities. For one thing, it is negative attention and the un-controlled child generally thrives on negative attention. Even when he sits in the time-out room he can—and does—imagine you are thinking of him. He may bask in the fantasy of your being consumed with thoughts of him and his suffering. Conse-quently, it is usually better to ignore provocative behavior when possible or to use some strategy short of the time-out room.

Secondly, some children use the time-out room to escape re-sponsibility. This must be interpreted to the child: "I guess you would rather sit in the time-out room than take a chance on doing such and such. Perhaps you are too afraid of what will hap-pen if you do a poor job."

Lastly, if the room is overused, it will have no impact. This is especially true with withdrawn youngsters, who hardly care where they are, anyhow.

STRATEGIES FOR THE
POORLY CONTROLLED CHILD

These ideas are designed especially for the poorly controlled child, but can be used with any child, according to the need. When you use these strategies, try not to imitate a therapist. Don't give the impression that the child is your patient, and that you are giving treatment. No child (or adult) likes to feel that you occupy a superior position from which vantage point you have decided he is the "sick" one.

To use these suggestions effectively, you must be familiar with them and believe in them. If they do not seem reasonable to you, do not use them. For if you do not think they are sound, you will unconsciously convey your doubts to the child. If you do not expect to be believed, you won't be.

1. Structure things so that the child knows exactly what the routine will be, what to expect moment by moment. Poorly

controlled children should encounter as few breaks in routine as possible. There is plenty of time later to teach flexibility to these children.

2. Use the family council to establish limits and rules. These rules must be experienced as relatively impersonal. This is important. If a child breaks a limit, he should feel "I have gone beyond what is allowable here." He should not come to feel "I have succeeded in angering my mother."

It is time-wasting and nontherapeutic for a child to feel that limits depend on you personally, on your moods, whims, or general temperament. *For if he sees the limits as originating within you, or as a function of your mood, it will (justifiably) make sense to him to continue to direct his assaults at you personally.* If the rules seem impersonal, it will not seem worthwhile to engage you in pathologic interchanges. Furthermore, the impersonal tone helps him to incorporate the routine as his own, which reduces his inner disorganization. The family council makes the limits at least largely impersonal.

3. Stay attractive as a personality, physically and mentally. You must remain a figure with whom the child can forge a positive identification. In short, you must provide some sort of ideal for the child.

At a more practical level, you should be the kind of person someone would want to take orders from or want to please. If you turn into a nag, a shrew, a person who must scream to maintain order, who will want to listen to you, and who will care whether you like him or not?

Anything which weakens your own self-confidence lowers your therapeutic efficiency. Your place in the hierarchy in which you work or live should be firm and definite. No one should lessen your confidence when you are interacting with the children. If there is an explicit or implicit rift in the husband-wife relationship at home, especially if one mate subtly or openly derides the other, these suggestions will not work well.

4. Consider the following suggestions as to things you can say to

a provocative or poorly controlled child. The interpretations are arranged from the very general, meant to be safe and useful with all children, to the more specific. In some cases, the mild interpretations are too mild: to utter them would be a waste of time. And often it is necessary to delay using the more advanced interpretations until the child has shown a tolerance for the more general ones. You must gauge where to start in the sequence, and also when the situation demands skipping *all* the verbal interpretations and proceeding directly to more advanced, direct measures, such as the time-out room.

Start with the knowledge that every child can be helped by a short, simple statement about the child's immediate intentions, provided the statement applies to obvious behavior and not to the child's unconscious intentions. For example, you can always say to an unruly child, "You would rather call out now than work quietly." But to say "You are so angry that you keep trying to bother me" would be useless to the child initially.

Simple statements of fact come in two categories. There are the statements about the immediate situation such as "You would rather walk around now than work"; and statements about the child's feelings such as "You become upset whenever you have to give answers out loud."

The statements of apparent fact are used at the outset. The statements about the child's feelings are introduced gradually.

An obvious behavioral statement may be considered the mildest and most acceptable type of interpretation and can be used in any situation.

Suppose a child gets up and walks around the room when he should be doing something else. You may say, "You would rather walk around the room now than finish the poster."

If the child is not too disturbed, this simple statement may bring him back. If it does not, he will either ignore the statement or else answer something to the effect:

"Yes, I would rather walk around."

At this point, it would be proper to use more personal interpretations, referring to the child's obvious intentions or fears:

"I guess you are wondering if you will be able to do the work correctly. Perhaps you feel someone may laugh at you."

Once some sort of relationship has been established, introduce more personal statements gradually:

"You seem to become upset when you think there is any possibility of making a mistake."

"You are angry that I asked you rather than someone else to do this."

"You would like me to stop what I'm doing now and pay more attention to you."

"You feel you just cannot sit with the group anymore." (This may be especially appropriate for the child with weakened self-control.)

5. If these statements do not help, add the use of acknowledgments. Remember that it is always helpful to a child, no matter how disturbed he is, to feel understood. There is tremendous therapeutic power in acknowledging a hurt person's feelings:

"You are very angry right now." (Some professionals feel it is wrong to acknowledge the feelings of people who are suffering from overwhelming emotions such as rage. We have not found this to be so, even with psychotics.)

Acknowledgments are highly useful in situations where children are lodging complaints, either against you, their peers, their home, or school. Without acknowledgment, the situation might develop as follows:

"I don't see why Johnny is allowed to stay out more than I."

The parent explains:

"Well he's older than you and more responsible."

And a vicious cycle begins.

"That's not fair. If he can stay out that long, I can too."

"But you don't understand. He's older."

"It's unfair. If he can, so can I!"

"But I explained to you . . ."

And so it goes.

This whole argument can be avoided by jumping right to an

acknowledgment of feelings after the very first explanation. Let's see how the sequence would go now:

"I don't see why Johnny is allowed to stay out more than I."

"Well—he's older and more responsible."

"That's not fair. If he can stay out that long, I can too."

At this point cease justifying yourself and instead acknowledge feelings:

"You're upset and feel I'm unfair."

From this point on, confine your remarks to the child's feelings. That is the level at which the problem exists. It is unsolvable at the "rational level," and so the ensuing argument will be unending. No amount of rational explanation will satisfy a child emotionally upset. The route away from the bind is to help the child deal with his upset feelings.

Typically, the encounter will end vaguely. The child will still be upset, but much less so than he would have been were his feelings not acknowledged. Once you have acknowledged his upset, you can withdraw quietly and walk away.

With highly demanding, provocative children there are further statements that may prove useful. You can say:

"I'm not interested in playing this game in which you push me and I get mad. I don't want to play any longer."

In a few months, after the child accepts the other interpretations, you can give longer interpretations such as the following:

"You have gotten into a state where you feel that absolute emotional attention must be directed at you. You don't care if the attention is love or hate, just so long as it is directed at you and is strong. It annoys you so much when you don't have this attention, that you'll do almost anything to get it—carry on, yell, hit."

Remember, be prepared to be rebuffed or ignored at first.

Let us sum up. When a child is unruly, you remember not to blame yourself and hence the child. You try to remain calm and attractive. You speak in a flat, unemotional way. You begin with a simple behavioral statement: "You would rather walk around now than sit at the table." After the statement is made, you ignore the limit-breaking child and proceed with your activities. *This provides a face-saving pause in which the child can rejoin normal activities.* If it brings no results, you add a statement about the lad's obvious intentions or fears: "You are afraid you will be unable to do what you think is expected," or "You would rather I pay more attention to you." *You will be able to carry out this step effectively only if you are gauging the child's intentions accurately.* Again, redirect your attention to your own activities. Next, acknowledge the child's feeling: "You feel quite upset now and are not sure what you want to do. You would like to remain with the group, but you're not sure you can."

Almost all negatively behaving children have mixed feelings about their behavior; they want to do it and not do it. Hence it is always helpful to verbalize this confused state of affairs: "You want to join us and yet you don't want to."

Notice one important point. *You have at no time made any direct commands,* such as "Sit down this instant."

One of the surest ways to lose control of an individual or group is to give orders that can be ignored or deliberately disobeyed. And another way to lose control is to hurl direct challenges: "You just do that one more time . . ."

So avoid such direct confrontations.

When and if the child's behavior reaches unmanageable proportions, proceed with whatever limit has been decided upon by the family council.

The rules must be well known to everyone and clearly defined in advance. Each child should know the decision criteria that may induce his exclusion from the group.

But this should be a last resort.

Maintain a calm mood and persist with interpretations as long as possible.

Avoid direct challenges. Even if you have to send a child to the time-out room, tell him he is there to *try* to settle himself; don't *order* the settling. Structure the day to avoid run-ins. If you know a child has a short attention span, plan his day so as to acknowledge this fact. If you know a child explodes whenever he has to do a certain thing, try to structure things to avoid a direct clash.

The more you give orders that are ignored, the less your authority will be. So set up rules in advance through the council. And see to it that you and your mate aid each other in enforcement—calmly and impersonally.

Once the limits are made clear, stick to a series of interpretations with pauses between each successive step as you progress from simple behavioral statements to more personal statements about intentions or fears to acknowledgments of feelings, particularly of the child's tendency to want to cooperate and not cooperate at the same time. From here you can jump right to limit-setting strategies, if you need them. You will have completely avoided the painful stage in which you bark commands or entreaties that are ignored.

6. If interpretations engender even more rage, persist with the general plan outlined. Do not get upset, and do not gloat that you are obviously right in your interpretation or else your child would not be upset.

If, however, your child flies into a really uncontrollable rage, attempt to hold him firmly and say, "You are unable to control yourself now, and so I will help you. I'll help you until you can do the job yourself." Only in extreme cases is it necessary for two adults to take hold of the child's limbs and carry him to the time-out room. One adult should be able to handle the situation.

7. Keep firmly in mind that there is only one reliable criterion of improvement in a disturbed child—*the frequency of his negative episodes*. This point cannot be stressed enough. A child who suffers temper tantrums five times a week may, after a lengthy period of exposure to this plan, suffer them only twice a week. Unless you are very perceptive, you may not recognize this as improvement. Most people watch and observe the negative act itself, rather than the frequency of the act. Most parents are so preoccupied with the fact that the child still has tantrums that they say to themselves, "The darn kid is just as

bad as he ever was!" and then return to their blaming and angry methods. It may take years for the negative act to fade out completely, but it should be infrequent by then.

Many parents (and therapists) have recognized what we call the Ping-Pong improvement effect. It is not unusual for a child, at least for the first few months, to get better and worse at the same time. What typically happens is this: the child's mood improves in a positive way; he "feels good" for longer periods of time. Yet his episodes become more intense than ever. The reason is that one part of his personality is being helped, but another part is afraid to abandon long-standing neurotic patterns, and so the fearful part tries even harder to reestablish the old neurotic patterns in which the child behaves poorly and the parents scream and shout.

8. In a home with many brothers and sisters, or in a school situation, the child may seek negative attention from his peers instead of from the adults in charge of him, especially if the adults have been successful in withholding their negative emotion.

There are a number of strategies available here. First, adhere to the general program outlined and maintain calm. Children actively seek to imitate those they admire and view as strong-willed. To the extent that you can remain calm and in charge will your position be unconsciously attractive to the child. If you become annoyed, and eventually enraged and disorganized when dealing with a provocative child, it will not be too long before your other children react in this same disorganized manner.

If you do have to make interpretations to your children as a group, say as you would to an individual, "I guess you're wondering just how far you can go—but this is not a game I wish to play"; "I suppose it's more appealing to you to do this [whatever the group is doing] than to take a chance on this work."

THE PLACE OF ANGER

Wherever we have spoken of our system, the response to its overall effectiveness has been consistently enthusiastic and positive, but one plaintive note has often crept in: Do we *really* mean parents should *never* be angry?

The answer to the question is Yes and No. No in the sense that no one (human) could ever achieve a state of complete lack of irritability, and besides, as we have seen, *some* anger is rational—anger in response to *genuine* attacks on life or life space. Nevertheless, Yes; anger should be maximally reduced because too many children thrive on it and hence actively seek it; and when they get it, they go after it again: in plain words, adult yelling increases rather than decreases children's problems. Furthermore, most anger is irrational and hence serves no purpose.

Remember that irrational anger need not be stifled or "swallowed," but can be handled by changing the irrational attitudes in whose name it is called forth—in short, by learning not to generate it in the first place.

Please note carefully again that anger and firm limits are not the same, and so when we say reduce irrational anger we are not saying be wishy-washy, overly permissive, or generally weak. As you have seen, our system depends on very firm limits, and on the parents being nonmanipulatable. *The aim is to stay warm as a person, but rocklike in not allowing yourself to be manipulated by poor behavior.* Should a child find he can use negative tactics to influence you, he will be in possession of a powerful weapon he is sure to use to your disadvantage.

Remember, too, that you cannot learn to reduce irrational anger overnight and that you will go through a long period of guilt and confusion before you achieve the goal. And so, do not vow to eliminate your irrational anger, but rather to strive to have less of it with each passing month.

THE PLACE OF POSITIVE EMOTIONS

We have, in all this, said nothing about your positive emotions: the love, affection, genuine empathy you show the child. We have covered only the elimination of the negative emotions. This has been deliberate, because if you feel little or nothing for your disturbed child, there is nothing we can do to change your feeling— except to remove the elements of self-blame, which may have been stifling positive reactions. *It is feasible and possible to help people stop blaming others, but it is quite difficult to induce love.* Therapists have known for a long time that it is much easier to remove negative blocks than it is to build responses that have been chronically absent. Witness the difficulty in treating psychopaths who lack the capacity to empathize with others.

Some parents (and even some teachers who deliberately *choose* to teach the emotionally disturbed) are *unable* to feel positively toward disturbed children. But whether a child is loved or not, his vulnerability to separation and to the absence of love *can* be reduced. (Though there are those who maintain that some youngsters cannot be helped *unless* they are loved. It is not certain whether this is so.)

12

The Total System in Use

Since parental insight, foundation skills, and the family council should be used together for the maximum effectiveness of the system, let us consolidate them by means of further examples. Note that in some cases a particular foundation skill may be emphasized.

Example 1. A six-year-old boy, prone to losses of self-control
Glen had two older brothers, a younger sister and a younger brother. His father was an engineer and his mother a warm, alert housewife. Psychological and medical testing of the child suggested a minimal form of central nervous system malfunctioning, although there was no known form of brain damage and no medication prescribed. The child was bright and could perform well in school when he maintained adequate self-control. But when frustrated, his self-directed anger became intense, and he dealt with this by turning it on whoever happened to be in the line of fire. He would act provocatively, tease, swear, and be surly.

His siblings were tolerant of Glen for the most part, although on occasion they would respond to his teasing with teasing of their own and sometimes with actual aggression.

His parents tried everything to reach Glen, from reasoning with him to bribing, hollering, and hitting. Everything worked—for about two days.

Parents do not typically seek professional help until they have exhausted their own resources, trying everything they have heard of in the way of child-management devices. (Unfortunately, they rarely stick to any one device long enough to allow it to work even if it could.)

Glen's parents were fairly reasonable, and had a good relationship as a couple. When we saw them it was not necessary to spend much time consolidating their relationship or their communication. We got right to work and taught them the system outlined in this book, with the emphasis on the family council to let Glen have a hand in deciding his limits and also to break up the hollering bouts between the child and his mother. (His father escaped those because he was away most of the time Glen was awake.)

Three things were especially important in working with Glen: (1) helping his parents learn not to relate to him through anger (we needed to reduce his addiction to negative attention, his wish for their anger); (2) helping them learn to set very firm and definite limits in order to afford them some protection from him, and to give him a definite set of boundaries he could depend on (we taught them not to back down on key issues when he yelled and became surly, for appeasement leads to blackmail); and (3) helping them learn to acknowledge the intense anger and frustration to which Glen was subjected.

We helped them to acknowledge Glen's fears that he could not function well in school and among his peers, and his new fears when he discovered that his tactics for securing negative attention no longer worked. The acknowledgments helped the boy develop a more realistic and tolerant picture of himself. Once he could see himself in more positive terms, he no longer had to become so enraged with himself and hence with others for real or imagined inadequacies.

Glen improved in the usual way. As the months passed and his parents remained firm yet nonblaming, Glen's periods of being out of control slackened. He still had occasional outbursts, even some intense ones, as he tried desperately to push his parents back into giving negative attention. But the severe outbursts were fewer and in time they ended, as he learned that his parents were not going to weaken.

When Glen could control himself, his school behavior and work were acceptable, and no further help was needed.

Example 2. A frightened and inhibited nine-year-old girl
Melissa had three older sisters, all of whom did very well in school. Melissa was only an average student and so felt inadequate and inferior to her sisters, all of whom teased her for her less-than-perfect performance in school and at play.

Her mother felt very guilty about the whole thing and unsure of what to do. She tried yelling at the older sisters, but that neither worked nor helped Melissa. The child resented her mother's running interference for her: she wanted to fight her own battles.

Melissa's father was a good provider, but totally disinterested in the children or their problems. Aside from telling his wife, "You're too nervous—that's all the trouble is," he did nothing for her or for Melissa.

Melissa became more tense with each passing year; her school grades dropped considerably. The family consulted us. At that point, it was a tossup as to what was causing most of Melissa's anxiety: her sisters' teasing or her mother's guilt and anxiety.

The family was unwilling to proceed with family therapy, the treatment we would have chosen so that the sisters and father could confront their negative contributions. The mother showed up alone for two interviews, and after that we talked to her by telephone.

Our first aim was to help the mother deal with her guilt. We explained that parents cannot be totally responsible for everything their children do, that it would be impossible for her to control each and every thing that might hurt Melissa: fate plays a large part in determining how children turn out. And we pointed out that sibling teasing is common.

We told Melissa's mother that if she could learn just one simple skill—how to make acknowledgments—she could help her daughter, regardless of the causes of Melissa's tension. It was impossible at the time to tell if this would be sufficient help for her child—Melissa's inhibitions might rest on a more complicated foundation and require more complicated treatment—but what her mother could do at home would help at least to some degree.

We suggested that when Melissa showed obvious tension, especially after her sisters teased her, her mother say simply, "I can understand how that feels—it feels bad when someone makes fun of you."

The mother wondered how such a simple thing could help, and so we told her of the tremendous healing potential in feeling understood.

We stressed that she need offer no false reassurances: " . . . but you shouldn't worry when your sisters tease you, honey, because you're really good in other things." Such sweet lemons sound phony because they are phony. There was no reason to be forced into lying about Melissa's competency. Such sweet lemons are not needed: when one human being feels understood and accepted by another, a goodly amount of the burden is lifted. Besides by trying to make "compensatory" remarks (" . . . you're really good at such-and-such"), the mother would merely convince Melissa more than ever that in her parent's eyes she was only as good as her accomplishments. This kind of thinking, carried to an extreme, can lead to underachievement, for if Melissa is only as good as her achievements, it may become too risky for her to try anything.

The acknowledgments would help Melissa fight her poor image and thereby reduce her resentment and hence her anxiety in relation to her sisters. And this strategy would provide the mother with something more positive to do for her daughter than to walk around with a long, guilty face.

In the second interview, we explained the family council to Melissa's mother and asked her to introduce it as fun—and not just a medium to criticize her husband and daughters. We told her to pay great attention to foundation skill 1, communicating without blame, in setting up the council, and to try to get her husband to join in gradually and eventually to lead.

A few months later we found that Melissa was less tense, and that the family council, although not working at maximum efficiency (the father's cooperation was still minimal), was doing some good. If nothing else, the mother felt less isolated and guilty. Melissa's sisters turned out to enjoy the council and were helping make it work.

Example 3. A disobedient fourteen-year-old girl, keeping company with a drug-using, law-breaking gang

Helen was a good-looking, auburn-haired girl, her father's favorite. Early in the game Helen had succeeded in weakening the parental relation. She had learned she did not necessarily have to obey her mother, because her father, who was away at the office all day and did not realize Helen's provocativeness, would intercede in her behalf.

In the process of trying to get Helen to obey, the mother turned more and more into a nagging shrew. Her troubles with Helen preoccupied her night and day—such were the bonds of sick dependency between Helen and her mother. When the father did chance to see his wife interacting with Helen, he observed a whiny, yelling, totally pathetic creature.

Helen would accept fewer and fewer limits with each passing year. She eventually stopped listening even to her father, who finally agreed that a problem existed.

Luckily, Helen's parents were not too defensive once it was explained to them just what had happened.

The first job was to do a personality face-lift on the mother. It was essential she put aside her nagging, pathetic ways and become someone worthy of respect. This and strengthening the parental relation had to come before any work could be done with Helen.

The mother was advised to get a part-time job. (All her children were in school.) Not only would a job give Helen's mother something to think about besides Helen, but it would give her a new role-identity to function in. She had already lost faith in herself as a mother and as a person. When self-respect goes down, total care for the self goes down. She had become sloppy in her appearance and with her diet. A paying job would force her to interact with people at an adult level. She would become more attentive to herself. Not only would this help *her*, but it would also help her husband regain a husbandly interest in her.

The job would probably make her feel more competent as a person, since far more people are successful at their jobs than as parents. It is much harder to be a good spouse and a good parent than a good worker; a family makes far more emotional demands.

Once the mother had a job, we directed attention to discovering in more detail just what had happened to the parental relation. We traced Helen's development. The father saw how he unconsciously had helped Helen split the marital relation. The mother saw how she had let herself go downhill and thereby given Helen and her father further excuse to denounce her.

Helen's parents introduced the family council idea at home. To their surprise, Helen accepted the idea. We told her parents to set firm limits together and to acknowledge Helen's ensuing frustrations. We encouraged them to follow foundation skill 3 and grant appropriate independence—appropriate to what Helen could handle.

As Helen found herself faced with a united front and unconsciously saw her mother as more worthy, she became better able to accept limits. Because the mother no longer forced herself upon Helen aggressively, Helen did not have to reject her aggressively (and totally).

Helen's parents were amazed to find that rules previously ineffective in guiding Helen's behavior had new authority behind them. Helen felt the commitment and sense of unified purpose in the parental approach, a unity that appealed to her unconscious need for parental strength.

Family and individual strength increased together. Helen was able to give up her law-breaking friends. She now derived enough strength from her family not to need these "friends."

(Whether or not a basically good child will be able to give up undesirable friends is hard to predict. A number of variables are at work: Are the pals *really* bad or is parental judgment faulty? Are there areas of life in which the child is competent aside from gang life? Have the parents left the child room for a positive identification—or have they made the child feel that to remain out of a gang would be equivalent to psychological suffocation, that having to accept any particular parental wish is symbolic of total domination?)

Example 4. A passive-aggressive eleven-year-old boy, well-behaved except at schoolwork

Jack had two older sisters who did average work in school. He was the first boy in the family. His father had high hopes for him, and from the beginning put him under pressure to do well in school. Jack did well in the early grades. But starting with junior high, where he had to change classes and in general act in a more adult fashion, his work began to slip. He became a dreamer. Since he was likable, his teachers gave him extra help. Then his work showed improvement, but it reverted when the tutoring stopped.

Through it all, he developed a passive-aggressive personality. He could not express his resentments openly and so expressed them by slowing down. Although not outwardly defiant, he irritated his parents because the things they asked him to do never got done.

Jack's parents had a good relationship with each other, although his mother sometimes accused his father of riding the boy too hard. He, in turn, felt she was too easy on him.

We explained our system to them and asked that emphasis be placed on the family council to encourage Jack to set up his own schedules for chores and homework.

Jack was glad to set up the homework schedule, but, of course, he did not follow it. With this, his parents said, "Jack, this is your own system. It's not working. We're going to have to ask you to design another."

His parents made other interpretations to encourage independence: "Jack, you are trying to force us into accepting your responsibilities. We do not want the job."

And they interpreted his resentment: "We can understand that this whole thing makes you very angry. After all, we *are* putting you under a lot of pressure although we don't want to. It's just that we also don't want the job of pushing you through life."

After a few weeks had passed and Jack had shown an ability to accept the above interpretations, they pointed out his fear of independence, based on a desire to remain a child: "The part of you that does not want to grow up *wants* us to order you around and take charge of you."

Jack's current tutors were encouraged to make the same interpretations.

The entire program required about one year to implement fully. There were frustrating failures along the way, as Jack designed systems he did not follow. But as of the latest information, Jack's grades have risen dramatically. It is too soon to tell if the positive changes will be permanent; there is a good chance they will be.

Example 5. A neurotic twelve-year-old boy who imagines he is very sick

Jerry's father was an intelligent and able physician; his mother, a controlling, domineering, bright and alert woman. His father imagined he had all kinds of dire illnesses and spent much of his time consulting other physicians. But his sense of duty prevented him from remaining away from work. Jerry's imaginary illnesses made him miss a great deal of school.

Jerry had an older brother and sister, both away at college, both doing well.

Our therapeutic job was carried out in two stages. At first we saw Jerry alone, our purpose being to get him back in school. In the majority of cases, if a child's symptoms keep him from attending school, it is a good idea to encourage him to return as soon as possible. Not only does this prevent his nonattendance from becoming a habit, but it also keeps him from losing too much schoolwork. (If, however, the illness rests on an underlying psychosis, it is not always wise to push for an immediate return to school.)

We showed Jerry how his illness was actually an attempt to

maintain a dependency relation with his mother, to whom he had become addicted. Although he accepted this interpretation somewhat skeptically, he did return to school. The early days of treatment were punctuated with anxious calls from his mother, wondering if she shouldn't keep him home from school after all because " . . . he really does seem to be in pain." Since medical examination uncovered no illness, we advised that this would be a mistake.

We told the mother that although she should acknowledge Jerry's pain—"Jerry, I *believe* you are in pain; I don't think you're lying"—she should remain unmoved by his symptoms and should tell him, "Even though you are in pain, we feel it would be a mistake to have you stay home and lose further confidence in yourself." Note that she never accused Jerry of lying or said his pains were not real. The hypochondriac as well as the psychosomatically ill person feels real pain. Too many patients and doctors think psychologically induced pain is somehow not real or hurts less than physically induced pain. This may be so, but it seems unlikely. Pain is pain: it hurts.

When his parents acknowledged Jerry's plight it was to let him know they realized he was in pain and was unhappy, but at the same time knew his eventual recovery demanded they not bow down to his fears.

After Jerry returned to school, we saw the entire family. We tried to show how the mother had bred dependence in both her husband and son—her own sense of self-worth demanded that someone or everyone need her—and how they constantly sought her maternal omnipotent protection through the development of symptoms. We showed the mother that although it may be fun to be depended upon some of the time, it certainly isn't fun in the long run, especially when she finds that her husband has turned into an emotional baby.

The family therapy portion of the treatment went on for more than a year. Jerry's symptoms faded, and his father showed more vitality, but at the time the treatment stopped the father was still much the same as he was when it began: this was apparently a comfortable personality for both him and for his wife.

We advised both parents to pay special attention to skills 3 and 4, encouraging independence and acknowledging feelings.

TO SUM UP

It is difficult to tell what portion of our overall system will help your family the most. It is best to do the preliminary work of ferreting out and changing those forces disrupting parental unity, then learn the basics (the foundation skills and the council), and proceed to use the system as a whole. As time passes, you will see which aspects seem to make the greatest contributions.

If the system does not seem to work, there is trouble either in the first stage (parental unity) or the second (the foundation skills). Professional help may be needed by some couples to complete the first stage, but for most couples it will be unnecessary. Just remember that health and insight are matters of relative degree and are not absolutes.

PART THREE

FROM BIRTH TO TEEN-AGE

13

The Child
from Birth to One

We have presented an entire system to use with various family problems, mild and serious. At this point, we would like to go back to a child's very beginnings, and trace his development year by year to show how the system outlined is relevant to the problems attending specific ages.

THE IMPORTANCE OF
KNOWING WHAT TO EXPECT

With all the potential problems to contend with, it is silly for parents to add others that can be easily avoided. And a whole set of headaches can be avoided if only each parent, particularly the mother, will take the time to learn what to expect of a child as he grows up. For much of what is normal will appear otherwise to the unprepared parent.

The baby cries for no apparent reason. Is this normal? How long should it go on?

The baby has always been placid. Suddenly his personality changes. He is frightened with strangers. He screams for his mother. Is this normal? If so, how long will it last?

There is little chance of staying sane unless you know what to expect of your children: which patterns to shrug off and which to take seriously.

Sunday supplement writers, including so-called experts, who try to convince you that rearing children is instinctive are, in our opinion, wrong. There is no reliable way to pick up information out of your psyche unless someone has put it there. Perhaps there is a maternal drive, and perhaps it motivates a mother to be kindly disposed and attentive to her children. But no specific knowledge is implanted. And though common sense and intuition are needed to rear children, they cannot substitute for hard facts.

In previous generations, knowledge of child rearing was passed down from grandmother to mother to daughter, all of whom lived in the same house. Today, the family is fragmented and the knowledge comes from outside.

The best way to become acquainted with your young child is to read one or more of the standard baby books, Dr. Benjamin Spock's *Baby and Child Care* or the *Better Homes and Gardens Baby Book*.

DEVELOPMENTAL SEQUENCES

A developmental sequence spells out the various stages of behaviors and attitudes through which children pass. But it is based ultimately on statistical generalizations, and so any departures of your child from this average sequence need not be cause for alarm. If your child's development is significantly out of tune with written developmental accounts, take this to mean that a closer look is needed and ask your pediatrician to investigate or make appropriate referrals.

Many researchers have noted that although the developmental sequence itself is rather similar from child to child, there is wide variability in timing. In other words, each child passes through stages a, b, c, d, etc., but child #1 might hit b, c, and d at very different ages from child #2. The children eventually travel the same ground but at different paces, and there is wide latitude as to what constitutes a normal or average pace. Some of the behavior considered average for the two-and-one-half-year-old may occur in a rapidly maturing child at age two, and that which is typical for the three-year-old may happen at two-and-one-half.

Some parents are quite adept at handling problems of a certain age, but cannot deal with those of another age. A mother may deal perfectly adequately with very young infants, but later be unable to cope with the normal defiance or willfulness of the typical two-and-one-half-year-old. Some parents are taken aback by the normal separation anxiety of the eight-month-old and react inappropriately, perhaps by becoming overly affectionate and manipulative, perhaps by rejection.

Should a normal developmental trend be reacted to too much or too little, the foundation is set for future difficulties, for either of these reactions stamp in or at least prolong behavioral patterns that would ordinarily be abandoned by the normally developing child.

Some expected negative behavioral patterns prove particularly difficult for *certain* children to shake off, and if their parents under- or over-react, the passing phase can become a permanent orientation.

A normal development may interact with an act of fate to produce a serious problem where normally none would have existed. If, for example, by some malignant stroke of fate, a mother dies when the child is in the normal eight-month separation-anxiety period, the child could suffer major psychological damage. Of course, the death of a mother is always tragic. The point we make is that what may constitute a "normal" trauma at one age may precipitate a serious and chronic crisis at another.

Frances L. Ilg and Louise Bates Ames in *Child Behavior* were impressed with the way some psychological patterns repeat themselves as children grow from two to sixteen. The basic sequence runs from a good, stable, balanced orientation to a rather poor, disorganized orientation; to a well-balanced pattern; to a very introversive orientation; to an extroverted, expansive pattern; to a less outgoing, more obsessive pattern; and back to better-balanced stability. This sequence plays itself out first between ages two and five, repeats itself between ages five and ten, and once again is manifested between ages ten and sixteen.

For example, the two-year-old has a good stable orientation. The two-and-one-half-year-old child is more disorganized and harder to handle. Three is a balanced sort of age, easier to work with. The three-and-a-half-year-old is characterized by a turning inward; he is unstable and on the fearful side. The four-year-old moves into a very expansive orientation. The four-and-one-half-year-old is less outgoing and easily upset. The five-year-old is characterized by greater stability. The cycle then begins again at five and one half.

We find this sequence much easier to observe in younger children, those between the ages of two and ten, than in older ones, but on a statistical basis, this sequence can be considered true or accurate.

EMOTIONAL DEPRIVATION

The most serious problem for the infant is complete emotional deprivation. Children under six months who are institutionalized become very listless and emaciated. They frequently fail to gain weight. They are unmoving and apathetic. Their bowel movements are more frequent than normal. Even their sleep patterns are not as good as those of normal children.

Treatment for such cases is difficult. Efforts need to be exerted to help the child develop a good relation with a mother figure. This person must be exceedingly patient and nonblaming, since children who were severely deprived emotionally as infants rarely develop without troubles. They reject love, though inwardly craving it. It is as though they must put any potential giver of love through a severe test: "I will not love you until you prove you will not desert me no matter what I do." They throw favors and treats back in the faces of those who offer them.

Many well-meaning parents who have healthy families decide to adopt a child with a deprived and traumatized background in order to offer the love and security of their home to an unfortunate. But often in a few years, the parents end up in a therapist's office—confused and angry. They thought the child would welcome their love and, instead, he has hurled it back. They feel the situation is unfair to their other children, because all their attention goes to the "bad one," who goes on causing trouble. Unless parents like this can be made to realize the child *does* want their love but fears he will be hurt again, things will come to an unhappy conclusion. It is exceptionally important for the parents of a deprived child to learn to set limits nonblamingly, and to take the apparent rejection of love impersonally. The child does appreciate their love and attention but must show hostility to the world.

THE OUT-OF-PHASE MOTHER AND CHILD

Certain mothers and children seem unable to hit it off together from the beginning. The child wants to sleep when the mother would like him to remain awake. She wants him to eat when he isn't hungry. He hits periods of maximum activity when she would like to sleep. And so it goes. This is the kind of situation of which a mother later says, "The kid has been impossible from the very beginning. There was no pleasing him from the time we got home from the hospital."

There seem to be three categories of out-of-phase situations.

One is populated with mothers suffering deep fears of maternal identity. Such women find it frightening at an unconscious level to do some important things associated with child-rearing like remaining in a giving frame of mind even when put upon, or doing without time of their own for lengthy periods. Mothers in this category usually have unpleasant pregnancies: more-than-average nausea, pain, or excessive staining. Out-of-phase situations based on a fear of maternal identity often require professional handling, since these mothers may become either very depressed as child-rearing responsibilities increase or else totally rejecting.

Another category of out-of-phase reactions includes those mothers who approach child rearing with storybook expectations. The baby will be beautiful, smile perpetually, be grateful for all the nice things Mommy does. Reality is rarely like this, and so, in her frustration, the mother becomes less and less able to gauge the child's real needs. She resents him for bursting her balloon of fantasy, for depriving her of her dreams.

The third category of out-of-phase situations concerns mothers and babies who have very different personalities. The baby may be a "hyper" child: fast, agile, ever-moving. The mother may be slow, phlegmatic, indecisive. Or the child may be slow, require long periods of time to eat, while the mother is the "quick type," anxious to get to other duties.

Out-of-phase situations are high-risk ones in that they can permanently sour child-mother relations. In most cases, though, the parent responds well to counseling. Very often all a mother needs is an explanation of what has happened, why things seem really worse than they are, and how she can, by relaxing, help to prevent further difficulties. Moreover, she has to be shown how with modest readjustment she can become more attentive to the child's *real* needs. Often she merely has to change some preconceived ideas to which the child has not conformed. In more severe cases, psychotherapy is used to help the mother tolerate the identity status of "mother."

EATING AND RELATED PROBLEMS

Most eating problems occur at two periods: with the introduction of solid foods, and at the end of the first year (or beginning of the second) when the child's appetite undergoes a natural decrease and the mother panics, thereby beginning an endless cycle of anxious attempts on the mother's part to overfeed, and rejection of food or eventual overeating on the child's part.

The following list covers most of the common complaints:

The voracious child: This child is a problem only when the mother becomes frightened. Very often a mother will describe her child as "voracious" because of her own fears and fantasies. Consult your pediatrician if you are worried about this, and a psychotherapist if you are greatly worried.

Refusal to eat: The child may refuse to eat for many reasons: allergies, wrong-sized nipples, etc. Many of the difficulties in this category demand medical attention. But our interest is with the mother whose child refuses to eat because of the mother's tension.

Such a mother should read Chapter 4 very carefully, for very likely she is engendering needless anger and hence anxiety in relation to the child or her marriage. Either that or she just lacks facts about children's appetites and imagines children are supposed to eat more than is really necessary.

Many losses of appetite are temporary. The main task is for the mother not to upset herself and thereby transform a minor and temporary problem into a chronic one. Pediatric reassurance is very helpful. But it is amazing how many mothers will still complain that their children are not eating enough even *after* their pediatricians have assured them weight gains are normal. These mothers betray their own fears or imagined inadequacies.

Colic: The main comfort for the parent with a genuinely colicky infant is that he will outgrow it. Almost all authorities believe colic fades out after the third month. It is normal for a baby to have one period of discomfort during each day. This is not genuine colic.

Additional suggestions: Let your pediatrician assure you the situation is not serious; work on reducing your own tensions via the material offered in Chapter 4; get out of the house as much as possible; do not guiltily assume you are responsible; guard against rejecting yourself and your child.

Transitions from breast or bottle to cups, then solids: A mother makes three mistakes: she fails to distinguish whether her child is the type of child who makes optimal transitions rapidly or gradually; she forces the child to make the transition when she has decided he should, rather than when he is ready; she mistakes momentary fretfulness or sorrow for trauma and assumes the child is going to give her a perpetual hard time, and so backs away from the change and allows the child to gain control over her.

Suggestions: Decide whether your child is the type who does better when he is confronted with a new situation at once or gradually. Most children do better on a gradual basis. If yours does, too, give him a little bit of new along with lots of the old as the first step.

Gauge from his general deportment when you think he is ready to take a transitional step. What is his general level of cooperativeness? Have things been going smoothly for a while? Do not introduce changes in times of stress. Children should not have to cope with too many new things all at once.

Almost all children will resist the cup initially, and later almost all will have mixed feelings in moving from liquids to solids. Expect him to push the strange items out of his mouth. Do not be upset by mild "sorrow" on his part. Do not assume he is picky and has strong likes and dislikes to which you must cater. So many lifelong food fads are begun because the young child bamboozled his parents with minor fretfulness. (But, if your older child already has a food fad and is otherwise healthy, ignore the fad. We are concerned here only with the introduction of foods.)

Serious eating problems: If the child refuses to eat at all or chews his food endlessly without swallowing, tell your pediatrician. A complete evaluation is indicated, including an in-depth interview with each parent.

Developing self-feeding habits: As soon as the child has reliable finger-thumb opposition and has either some teeth or strong gums, he is ready for finger-feeding. This will usually be somewhere toward the end of the first year. Overly fussy parents botch the job badly (and usually go on to botch encouraging independence). You must accept the fact that the finger-feeding child is going to be sloppy. Do not hover and do not wipe him every time food gets on him, which will be every time. If you do, he will give up self-feeding and start developing the difficulties of the child lacking independence.

Pacifiers: Experts and lay people do not agree on the use of the pacifier. We feel that if the child does not have an intense need to satisfy the sucking urge, why bother with a pacifier? On the other hand, if regular feeding activity does not satisfy his sucking needs, why not use one?

If you do give him one, do it *after* he has eaten, *if* he shows that he still has a strong urge to suck. Take it away from him as he is falling asleep. In this way, he will not come to depend on it. But, if he is already dependent on it, don't worry: he'll outgrow it; besides, you still have control over where and how it can be used.

Constipation: Consult your pediatrician. Parents make one huge psychological mistake in this area. They allow the child's bowels to become a focal point for them and for the child. Guard against this. Do not stamp in what would be temporary. The child's bowels are hardly a worthwhile or invigorating focal point.

Baby-sitters: Do not be afraid to leave your young child. It is good for you, and for him. But ask the baby-sitter to observe not only your rules but also your rhythms.

Do not be fooled by normal periods of separation anxiety. Talk soothingly to the child, but depart when the time has come. Don't feel guilty, and try not to communicate any upset.

Head-banging, rocking, etc.: There is a wide variety of behavioral patterns for which no clear meanings have been established: head-banging, excessive rocking, breath-holding, some forms of vomiting, thumb-sucking, lip-pulling, hair-twisting. These patterns are sometimes observed in children encountering all sorts of difficulties and sometimes in children who develop without incident. Not only is it not clear what these patterns mean, but it is uncertain whether they should be considered warning signs. It is best to have your child's physician render an opinion.

There are various theories put forth to explain the phenomena. Some theoreticians feel that head-banging and body-rocking are attempts on the part of the child to establish or strengthen what are technically called his body boundaries. In their opinion, the child has an ego disability that makes him unable to form a coherent image of himself, and unable to integrate physical movements and behavior. So he bangs and rocks to compensate for the disability.

Children have few ways to express their frustrations and rages, and so the banging, rocking, breath-holding, etc., may represent attempts to discharge rage, perhaps rage which for one reason or another has built up to excessive intensity. Or perhaps the child's normal routes of discharge are, for some reason, inhibited.

Try your best to gauge your child's need accurately. In this way you can reduce at least some of the frustrations which produce rage. But most important, don't panic, and don't allow yourself to be manipulated. Stay calm, and proceed with whatever limits may be needed in a given situation. If the action is dangerous, as is head-banging, tie pads to the crib boards and sides. With some activities, such as rocking, there may be nothing to do except wait until the child outgrows the pattern.

In some few cases complete medical, neurological, and psychological evaluations are warranted. Allow your physician to help you make this decision.

MARITAL DEMANDS OF THE NEW PARENT

It is not unusual for new parents to try all kinds of nonsense on each other early in the game. The mother may refuse to go out, explaining she cannot leave her young child. Or she may refuse to have intercourse. "It will wake the baby. Besides, I'm too tired; you can't take care of the baby and still be interested in sex."

The father may insist the child be made to stop crying, and make his wife feel this is her lifetime job: to protect the father from ever being annoyed by the children.

Such irrational demands, on either side, had best be settled early in the game. Use all of the materials in Chapters 4 and 5 and/or get professional help. Child rearing founded on such a basis is doomed, as is the family which tolerates it.

14

From Age One to Three

Not everyone accepts the view that the childhood years are of decisive importance. Perhaps the position has been overstated. The best view is to be had in Erik H. Erikson's *Childhood and Society* on which the following account leans heavily.

It is certainly *not* true that important changes are *never* possible once a personality has matured. And it is almost never true that a person is forever *doomed* by negative childhood events. But it *is* true that no other sequence of years rivals the early ones in total importance.

Just consider the important issues to be settled in childhood. The first and most basic issue is whether life itself will be seen as worth the while. The child must decide on whether or not he can depend on what is "out there." He gradually knows "something" is; and that whatever this something is, it is responsible for his comfort and safety—indeed for his very survival. To the extent that a mother can accurately gauge her child's real needs—can differentiate, say, hunger from sleepiness or from overtiredness and hence can respond to these *real* needs—will he form the belief that what is out there can be trusted, and is therefore good and worthwhile.

The child must then face the issue of whether *he is good.* This is determined in largest part by the attitudes his parents harbor toward him as shown by the way they respond. Are they warm? Accepting? Friendly? Or hostile and rejecting? Do they make demands the child can meet, or do they demand the impossible, by insisting that he do what he is not yet ready to do: toilet train before he even understands what is expected; share his belongings before he has even consolidated his sense of ownership. Do they thwart him in his every bid for independence? Does he encounter No! with everything he seeks to touch? This will make him permanently distrustful of his own willpower, forever afraid to be truly independent.

Next, the child must decide how productive he can safely be, what sense of initiative he can display. Will he be thwarted or encouraged by his parents?

We certainly do not imply that parents are *solely* responsible for the development of these skills or abilities. We do mean, however, that parents play important roles in the development of the young child's accomplishments. And we mean also that parents should not expect children to mature in nice, even, smooth-climbing progressions. A child goes over mountains and down valleys of development: his progress is followed by seeming setbacks. From acting friendly and mature, he may become a reclusive tyrant—and still remain within the bounds of the expected.

A QUICK LOOK AT THE YEARS
FROM ONE TO THREE

Motility dominates the picture: the child wants to get around.

The next most noticeable thing may be the two periods of negativism—around eighteen months and around two-and-one-half years—that the child passes through.

At some point he must be toilet trained.

He will form and begin to use language skills.

From being self-centered he must begin to learn to get along with others.

Most critically during these early years, the child must form an attitude toward his own willfulness—his willpower. These are the years the child consolidates his knowledge that he is a separate person, that he can *will* things—*all by himself.* He doesn't have to await others. He tries out his willpower in all kinds of ways. At times, he abuses the privilege by being negative, by refusing everything. How much can he get away with? What does he *have* to do, and what will get done to him?

These are agonizing times for parents and children. Can the child modify his desires to meet those of his parents? Or will he be so overwhelmed by unmet needs that he can't? Unsolved problems from one phase carry over to make problems at future phases. Should a mother fail to respond to her child's real needs, should she, for example, feed him every time he cries instead of seeking the true nature of his desire—which may be simply to be let alone—she will encourage the development of intense, chaotic, insatiable emotions. As a result, in his next phase of development, when the child must learn to modify some of his demands and hence regulate his willpower, he may have to deal with extraordinarily intense rather than normal emotions and desires.

As the parents try to help the child develop a proper sense of willpower, they must set appropriate limits, remain nonblaming and grant independence in such a way that the child is given a wide but not endless range of freedom. The parents' ability to do so will determine whether the child will enjoy an appropriately modified but not overly inhibited willpower, or will emerge paralyzed by a distrust of himself and his initiative. Will he be assertive—able to pursue what he wants with an appropriate degree of aggressiveness, or will he be anxiously submissive? Will he decide that his environment makes hopeless demands on him, and so take a permanently hostile point of view? Will he find he can act only through massive assertions of his will—that only by spasmodic, impulsive outbursts can he overcome the pileup of inhibitions his parents have handed him?

MOTILITY

Motility, the ability to get about, can provide the child with a vast panorama of exciting exploration and discovery or a battleground of frustration, anger, and anxiety. Nowhere will the nervous, fussy, overly protective parent so betray his true colors as here. Life can become a series of anxious No's for the child: endless warnings, constant pickings up, needless washings, needless removals of perfectly harmless objects—in short, a world in which individual initiative is not only unwanted but declared dangerously out of bounds.

The foundation skills are needed to meet the challenge of increasing motility. The parents must set firm but *appropriate* limits. These limits should encompass a wide area of freedom— but *must not* be endless. Just as a child can be hurt by too much oppression, so he can by infinite freedom, not only physically hurt, but also emotionally: an unbounded universe is overwhelming. An endless universe evokes endless longings, and endless longings overwhelm the personality's capacity to contain them. A lack of definite boundaries makes a child believe the endlessness is inside him and hence imagine he can be swamped by unbounded emotion.

But as we have stressed before, the limits are of little value if they are not set and maintained with some degree of calm. Should the child sense anger, blame, or anxiety behind the setting of limits, he will find the limits that much harder to accept. He senses your insecurity, and hence knows that these areas are areas of personal vulnerability. Remember that the purpose of the limit is to have the child eventually accept the limit inwardly. Children are unlikely to accept limits about which you yourself harbor doubts.

It is easiest to maintain a nonblaming calm if, as we suggested, you childproof your house. Take advantage of every mechanical contrivance you can to set up the house so that it minds itself: plastic inserts for electrical outlets, locks for cabinets—including a belt lock for under-the-sink cabinets containing poisonous chemicals—gates for dangerous stairs, locks for all doors, especially bathroom doors. Remove all knickknacks. As we noted, you can teach the child respect for such things later, when respect is easier to teach. Forget about the warnings of those who believe the child will grow up a social boor if his hand is not constantly slapped for touching an endless array of stupidities, like ashtrays. Unless you want a war in which everyone loses, childproof your home.

There will be times when the child *must* be frustrated. After all, there are things in the house that cannot be roped off, and there are treasures that cannot be mechanically placed out of bounds. While you are carting him away from the TV set, a gentle but firm "I know you're upset but you may not touch that" will work just fine even if the very young child does not understand each word. He will understand your mood. Don't forget acknowledgments of feeling.

We have said nothing about the foundation skill of encouraging independence, because the child's inborn quest for this treasure is at an all-time high during these years. His motility—crawling, walking about, touching, smelling, mouthing—all of these are the foundation stones of independence.

If the Child Does Not Accept Limits

If a child does not accept limits on his motility, if he continues to touch things that are out of bounds, there are a number of possibilities to consider. Perhaps there have been too many No's: this is most frequently the culprit. If you load your child up with No's, he soon tunes you out. He reasons that your demands do not make sense and are not consistent. So he throws out the entire package, your good and worthwhile limits along with the nagging, silly ones. Rethink your outlook. Try not to see the world as a catastrophically dangerous place. Ask yourself if your list of No's is really appropriate. See if perhaps you do not have too many negatives. A few limits, absolutely essential, are much easier to enforce than a long list, sporadically enforced.

The next most frequent reason why young children do not accept limits is that the parents have not persisted to the point where the child can incorporate them. A great deal of patience is required. When you are setting a limit as to where the child can go, do not start out believing a previously uncontrolled child will listen to you the first time around. Start out rather with the inner pledge that *you will persist through as many trials as are necessary* for your child to learn what is appropriate. In this way you will not be disappointed with yourself when the child fails to accept the limit. Once you make the vow, the child will sense your will-to-victory and will probably accept the limit. It is when parents show disgust too rapidly that the child knows he has won the battle.

There are some rare and special conditions under which children cannot accept limits on early motility patterns, conditions involving mild or serious brain damage. Professional help is needed for these, but the system will aid these children also. Add more childproofing to the home. Be as patient and as firm as necessary. There are no magic ways to help a child achieve adequate control of his motility. Drugs may help in some very special cases, but with these children as with all others, nothing can substitute for nonblaming, appropriate limits, encouragement of independence, and acknowledgment of frustrations.

LEARNING TO LISTEN

In a later chapter on the immediate preschool years we will review many of the things you can do to help your young child to learn more effectively. But there is one thing you can do right from the start: learn to talk to the child an appropriate amount of time—not too much and not too little—and learn to pay genuine attention to what he says, at least sometimes. Now it is perfectly true that some children are chatterboxes even early in the game, and no one could really listen to all they have to say. But whatever time you can muster to pay real attention will be profitable. Nothing develops language arts so much as the conviction that what one has to say is worthwhile. Only when a child feels he has, at least some times, a *genuine* audience, will it make sense to him to continue developing his language skills. There is an indirect bonus here, for current research proves that the amount of genuine interaction between a mother and a very young child is positively correlated with later intelligence.

NEGATIVISM

As we have mentioned, at approximately eighteen months of age, and again at two-and-one-half years, the child normally passes through a phase in which he is intensely negativistic: contrary and rebellious. These are also the ages, particularly at two and one half, when his ambivalence is extreme: he holds two mutually exclusive desires at the same time and yet feels they are both essential, that he would sacrifice something vital if he abandoned either one of them. And so the ambivalent child clings tenaciously to irrational and painful indecision.

"I want to play with that toy myself." "I want to give that toy to my brother."

"I want to go with you to the store." "I don't want to go with you to the store."

That is how the ambivalent child would verbalize his feelings were he able to translate them into words.

There is one main danger to which parents are exposed while their children are passing through stages of ambivalence: the danger that the negativistic behavior may become "stamped in," chronic—if parents do not set proper limits in a nonblaming way. Some parents wrongly assume that normal negativism is the start of some chronic pattern and that they must immediately take a hard stand against it. In their panic to stifle any sign of rebelliousness, they resort to hostile anger and blame, and an endless cycle of punishments.

Once a child is overly punished, he forms the idea he is no good. Some parents even encourage this idea by *telling* him he is no good: "From the time that damn kid was eighteen months old he's been bad!" As we have seen, once a child has a label foisted on him, he has a perverse way of living up to that label. The process is unconscious; the child rarely knows this is what is happening. When a child knows or senses that he is considered bad, he will continue to act in ways he believes bad children should act.

Overpunishment acts in more subtle ways to encourage negative behavior. The child comes to feel he is only safe when he is being punished, for he feels, unconsciously, that his parents *prefer him* in a state of being punished. To insure the continuance of this assumed-to-be-preferred state, he begins to *seek* to be punished. Yet at the same time, another part of his personality resents the punishment, and so increases his need for revenge.

This sequence is one of the routes to the development of a need for negative emotion. The child relates to people through seeking to evoke their negative reactions.

Overpunishment is not the only way a normally developing behavioral sequence can be stamped in or perpetuated long beyond the time it would ordinarily have faded out. Some parents are so upset at the child's negativism that they employ an endless parade of deceits to manipulate him. They try to seduce him or to ask him to do the opposite of what is really wanted. In this last maneuver they are supported by the otherwise sensible team of Frances Ilg and Louise Bates Ames who in *Child Behavior* tell parents: "Don't be above using guile." Of course there is nothing wrong with being wise enough not to give the child too many choices to begin with. But in our opinion deceitful manipulations—such as telling the child the opposite of what you really mean—are not helpful in the long run, for once parents start using them they don't know when to give them up and turn to honest firmness.

The "over" reactions—overseduction, overaffection, overmanipulation—generally produce more complications than they settle: the overly seduced child develops a longing for union with his mother which may haunt him the rest of his life. The child who is given affection as a device to end his negativism generally becomes addicted to the affection and so may continue the unwanted behavior merely to get this craved-for response. The overly manipulated child rarely becomes appropriately independent and instead passes from the negativistic stage into a whiny, demanding, tearful, obnoxious stage that may last a long, long time.

Next to overpunishment, the most frequent mistake parents make when dealing with a negativistic child is to bite at all the bait he dangles in front of them.

"I'm not going to pick up the toys," states the child.

"What do you mean you're not going to pick up the toys? You have to pick them up. What's the matter with you, can't you ever do anything you're asked?"

Had this mother waited, the child would probably have done his picking up, even while maintaining his arch resistance at a verbal level. Far too many parents create an agitated verbal world for themselves and their children by responding to each and every little thing said.

Be assured: *the great majority of negativism can be handled by the simple art of ignoring.*

Foundation skills 1 and 2 will be of great help in dealing with your negativistic child. Do not become hostile by assuming the child is willfully being negativistic for the sole purpose of getting at you. And do not be misled into overlooking appropriate limits. Don't offer him too many choices, and in many situations offer him no choice at all. If he does not do what is required, simply pick him up or walk him through the activity with the simple statement, "You have to do this."

TOILET TRAINING

Toilet training means different things to the mother and the child. To the mother it means the end of a lot of unpleasant jobs and therefore something to look forward to. To the child, it represents giving up important parts of himself at the request of someone else: one more attempt to limit him and his freedoms. No wonder that so many mothers and children meet in armed battle at the potty chair.

When a mother is aware that what she is asking of her child is not easy and when the child has enough positive feelings to want to cooperate, the time is right for toilet training.

There are two stages of the training. In the first, the *mother* is trained: to recognize when the child needs to go to the bathroom. With some predictable and cooperative children this stage can be attained around the end of the first year.

In stage two, the child's voluntary cooperation is enlisted. He is encouraged to give the mother a signal. Most parents begin toilet training with stage two at around eighteen months to two years, depending on the cooperativeness of the child.

What procedure should you follow? First, take the child to the bathroom at regular intervals. You will know at what intervals from stage one, or from your current observation. Wait three to five minutes. Praise successes. Make no comment when there has been no success. If a later accident occurs, change the child without comment or blame. By following this pattern you will probably have a child who is trained by the time he is two and a half to three. (Mothers who brag their children were trained at one year mean *they* were trained; they mistake a stage one success for a stage two success.)

Within this whole period, accidents will happen. Visitors, strange houses, a new brother or sister, being outside at play—almost anything—can upset a routine only tentatively established.

When accidents occur, respond neutrally with "Soon, you will let me know . . ." And continue to praise successes.

When things go wrong during toilet training and a child is frightened by the sound of the toilet flushing or loss of balance, backtrack for a few days. Then start over as originally outlined.

In the case of severe tension, professional help in the form of parent counseling or a habit-retraining technique may be needed. But the child will still profit from this toilet-training procedure.

Night training is usually not achieved until after daytime training. But when a child over four or five is still wetting the bed, a medical check is in order. Any treatment plan must also insure that the child is not blamed for his problem, or embarrassed by it.

The application of foundation skills 1 and 4 are particularly important to toilet training. A child who is blamed for his accidents will continue to have them. And when things have gone wrong, it is most important that the child's feeling be acknowledged. Successful completion of toilet training is one of the most important steps in developing independence in the young child.

SLEEP PROBLEMS

Sleep patterns vary. The very young infant needs a lot of sleep, the older child less, but by no means in a set way. Not only are no two children alike, but the same person may show quite a variable pattern. It is wise for a parent to have some reasonable idea about the sleep needs of the young child. Many problems result from a parent's assuming that all her children are exactly alike in their sleep needs. A new mother may insist her child take a nap long after he has ceased needing one; she thereby starts not only a sleep problem—"That darn kid won't stay in bed"—but a behavior problem as well—"He just doesn't listen to me anymore."

Separation anxiety and neuroses in general may contribute to sleep problems, but frequently the problem occurs because a parent overreacts to what would have been a temporary upset. A minor medical problem, overstimulation, overexcitement caused by a form of masturbation—all of these may cause the upset. If the child is not overly neurotic to begin with, and if the parents do not overreact, these temporary stresses will disappear with the passage of time. But should the parents be unable to spot the trouble as temporary, and should they either blow it up or punish the child for "not going to sleep like a good boy," a chronic battle may start.

Some parents are unwise about bedtime, either insisting a child go to bed too early or forcing him to stay up too late. We almost had a sleep problem with two of our children because one of us (the father) used to arrive home very late at night and want to see them. They were kept up until we saw the handwriting on the wall and gave up this basically selfish practice. If you are erratic, inconsistent, or unmindful of your children's hours, you may start a problem where none existed before.

The best remedy for sleep problems is to avoid them by getting your child started with good sleep habits:

1. Read some of the standard baby books to find out about normal variations in sleep patterns.
2. Try to gauge your child's own needs for sleep. Do not be guided by what your mother or Aunt Nellie told you. Be guided rather by reality.
3. Establish a firm nighttime pattern with your young infant and try not to depart too radically or for too long a time from this pattern. When someone sits with your child, ask her to follow this same routine.
4. Be definite in your ways. Have faith that your will is going to prevail.

Countering Poor Sleep Habits

On no other battlefield is parental will-to-victory so important as in dealing with the child who refuses to stay in bed. It is not easy to stay calm after a child has cried out or come downstairs for the tenth time, especially when you are tired and are looking forward to some time to yourself. But you will succeed if you remember that your child will give up his demands for attention just as soon as he becomes firmly convinced he cannot win. Your anger, disgust, yelling, screaming, betray to the child one thing—that *his* victory is just around the corner, because you cannot take it much longer. Foundation skill 1, remaining nonblaming and calm, is essential to the parental will-to-victory in dealing with sleep problems.

Many parents of children with mammoth sleeping problems have scoffed at our strategy. How could the mere will-to-victory accomplish so much? After all, they would say, didn't we obviously want our children to stay in bed?

Yet our system has worked thus far with great success, every time the strategy is carried out calmly and nonblamingly.

Many cases of poor sleeping habits are based on genuine fears, and your calmness, combined perhaps with appropriate acknowledgment, will help reduce these fears, regardless of their genesis. But if your child cries repeatedly or shows intense distress, make sure to consult your physician.

Now as to the strategy itself:

1. Stick to the firm nighttime routine. Avoid overstimulation at bedtime. Put the child to bed with a great deal of definiteness, as though you expect things to go well, regardless of what has happened in the past, but make sure that the child's bathroom and water needs are provided for ahead of time.

2. Should the child scream, go back in and calm him. Pat his back; kiss him. Give him assurance. *Under no conditions take him out of the room, allow him to come into your room, or lie down with him.* The essence of curing a child of a sleep problem is to demonstrate that while you have great sympathy for his desires and/or fears, you have absolutely no intention of allowing him to gain anything by not staying in bed, and you will not let him link you into a game. You are not going to become snared in his web either by overconcern, overniceness, or anger, but you will help him deal with his fears by remaining warm, sympathetic, and acknowledging.

3. Reenter the room as many times as is necessary, even up to ten or fifteen times if he continues to scream in terror. Never stay more than a minute or two and never return in less than, say, five minutes. Simply go back in, pat his back, indicate you realize he's afraid (either by word with children or by tone with infants) and then leave. *It will help you stay calm and nonangry if you plan this as your evening's activity.* Even in severe cases, one or two nights will probably be all that are needed.

4. With children who repeatedly leave their rooms, the aim is not to make them fall asleep (which you cannot do anyway) or even remain in their beds. *The aim is simply to show them they cannot ensnare you into their activities:* hence it is enough to keep them in their rooms. If the child shares a room with a sibling, whom he awakens or annoys, you *may* have to make your goal keeping him in bed—or else change room assignments.

5. Night wandering is common and normal between three and four and is not part of a manipulative plan to ensnare parental attention. Make your house safe with the aid of a standard baby book.

6. With "mild" cases, tell the child he may take toys to bed with him, or have the radio on. "Honey, you can have toys or a radio, but you're going to have to stay in your room. I know you're afraid [or want something], but it will lower your confidence even further if we let you call on us all night. We're going to stand firm on this and not back down, no matter what."

With really severe cases, you may have to put a sturdy gate across the room entrance, so that you can see in, but the child cannot get out. Tell the child, "You can turn on the lights, play with toys, play the radio low, in short do anything you want—except bring us into this. That would just lower your confidence."

Since the child's real, if perhaps unconscious, purpose is to strengthen the dependency bonds between his parents and himself, he will not be interested in these "privileges" (radio, toys) for long. When he finds he cannot capture your emotional attention, the other activities will lose appeal. After all, the child *is* sleepy. If he's not, maybe his bedtime hour is inappropriate.

Since your child's erratic going-to-sleep patterns may be based on neurotic fears, your calm, nonangry approach is of crucial importance. Should the program not work within one or two weeks, consider seriously the need for a professional evaluation.

NORMAL FEARS

The standard baby books list many fears which are typical of the child between one and three years of age. They may appear very suddenly and seem so unbelievably intense that you will think he will never get over them. Yet if things are even approximately normal, your child *will* get over these fears, possibly as abruptly as they set in.

Some fears are particularly "normal" in the sense that most children harbor them for a time. At eight months you may note a sudden fear of strangers. Or the young child may fear he will wash down the drain with the used bath water, and hence will begin to scream at bathtime. The vacuum cleaner's noise may startle and then frighten him.

The fear of bathing can sometimes be handled by the use of a smaller tub inside the regular tub. The small tub makes the youngster's universe more finite and hence less frightening. In extreme cases, introduce the child back to bathing gradually. On the first night talk about bathing. Show him pictures of children bathing, and tell him that although he is afraid now, he will soon be over his fears. Wash him at the sink. The next night, tell him you would like him merely to *get in* the tub within a tub, but that you will not turn on the water. Again wash him at the sink. The third night put just a little bit of water in the tub, and the fourth a little more. Gauge the increase in water level by the degree of fear. The greater the fear, the less the increase each night. Have patience. Progress is very, very slow the first few nights. If you remain very calm and remember to acknowledge the fear, "I realize you're upset now, but you won't always feel this way," you will find that after the first few days of slight progress there will be a big jump in a positive direction.

Use foundation skills 1 and 4 with your child's other early fears. Stay calm. Never belittle the child for his fears or tell him it is senseless to have them. Such advice does not help *you* when you're afraid, and it won't help your child. Reflect and acknowledge the fact that he is afraid, and remind him he will not always feel this way. Most of the fears will fade out of the picture without your even being aware this is happening.

JEALOUSY

It seems to us that parents worry needlessly about the reaction of their young child to a new sibling. It is not that he doesn't have a reaction; he does, and it may be intense. But why such frantic efforts to deny the reality with which the child is faced? After all, there *is* a new sibling. This new sibling *is* going to get a good bit of available parental attention. It seems to us best for parents simply to let the older child suffer his miseries in peace, rather than belaboring him to help with the baby or to declare his love for the baby while visiting relatives and friends stand around applauding this demonstration of "spontaneous" generosity.

Treat the situation matter-of-factly and honestly. You have a new baby. You are happy—and you are going to show this happiness. Sure, encourage the older child to do a thing or two for the new baby if he wants to. But don't make either a ritual or a routine of it. And *do not* insist that the older child immediately love his new rival.

Continue to relate to the older child in a normal way. Give him the same love and attention he should be getting regularly. If he is overly jealous, you will find that his jealousy cannot be reduced by trying to make it up to him with extra affection. The more you overgive, the more insatiable he will become—and the more unhappy. An insatiable child will accuse you of doing more for the new child whether this is true or not. You will argue, "You ungrateful wretch—we do far more for you, and you don't realize it." When the child is haunted by a fear of losing your attention, you cannot mollify him with greater and greater amounts of attention, for his appetite for it grows even faster than you can feed it.

If your child seems overly jealous, you have likely failed in relation to foundation skill 3, the encouragement of independence. The overly jealous child needs to be weaned. He is already overly dependent. This is why he cannot adjust to the new baby. Read all the material on foundation skill 3 very carefully, and carry it out.

NAGGING AND WHINING: THE CONSTANT DEMAND FOR ATTENTION

The child who spends his day whining for attention has also been failed in relation to skill number 3, the encouragement of independence. It is also possible that skill number 2 was not carried out effectively, that limits were set too fussily and inconsistently.

The child who whines and nags is addicted to his mother. He believes he cannot live without her. He may also crave negative attention and hence aim for her anger and disgust. He acts as though he must have a certain amount of emotion and he doesn't much care what kind of emotion it is—affection or anger.

It is not always easy to help the whiny child overcome his difficulties, for very often his mother is that mother we mentioned earlier, the one with a deep-set belief that her children will drain her. She responds to this fear by overly feeding, giving, and manipulating her children. It is hard for this kind of mother to encourage independence. And yet that is the treatment of choice: foundation skill 3.

SHARING

We have already mentioned a rule we have at our house that what-is-yours-is-yours. No child ever has to justify his desire to take possession of one of his own toys—even if someone else happens to be using it at the time.

When we tell of this rule at various meetings, there is always an indignant gasp from someone in the audience who demands to know how we get our children to share their belongings if we encourage them in such despotic tyrannical ways. Part of our answer is simple. Sharing behavior cannot be taught—at least not directly. The ability or capacity to share is a by-product of an otherwise correctly lived life. If the child is not too full of conflicts, sharing will not be a big problem for him. But the child who has been overly intruded upon and hence has no conception of what safely belongs to him, who has been forced to share before he could consolidate his sense of ownership, the child who has a need to possess and manipulate his friends via his toys, *will* have a hard time sharing, no matter what orders you give him.

Before a child can share he must map out what belongs to him, what he can control via his own will, and what others may control at their will. Then and only then will he be able to part with his belongings, secure they will come back to him. The child whose parents have used deceit or have overly intruded on his life will be unable to share, for his parents have so manipulated his life that he isn't sure what he can trust and what he cannot trust. He isn't even sure how much of himself belongs to him, since his parents demand and control so much. Maybe *they* own him. He cannot let things long out of his grasp, for he has no way of knowing what will come back.

Here is how sharing behavior can be encouraged:

1. Observe foundation skills 2 and 3: make sure the limits are appropriate, and independence encouraged.

2. Let the child know that what is his is his. He can have it when he wants it.

3. When he refuses to share his toys with his peers, he will see that other children grow disenchanted with him. Instead of berating him with, "What did I tell you! Nobody will play with you. Nobody likes you," apply foundation skill 4.

A reflection is a simple and gentle thing, yet it is miles apart psychologically from screaming derision.

You could say simply, "I suppose it's very upsetting when you find children won't play with you when you don't share your toys."

The reflection will not work wonders the first time you use it. Your child won't answer; "Oh yes, Mommy darling. I see what a fool I've been. I must share my toys like a good little boy."

Your child may not even say *anything* after you have made the reflection. He may complain bitterly about his friends' unfairness. But the reflection still has one great advantage: it is not an accusation. It is only a confrontation with some aspect of reality. Psychologically, the child can pay attention to a reflection. Perhaps some hours after the incident, he can think to himself, "That's right. They won't play with me when I don't share."

4. The child who uses his toys to manipulate others has probably been overly manipulated himself. One or both of his parents have fallen down as regards skill 3, the granting of independence.

15

From Age Four to Five

There is tremendous variation as the child moves from age three to age five. The child at three is relatively tranquil, but at four he tests limits to the extreme. A good bit of the four-year-old's out-of-control behavior is not really meant for you personally, although it might seem so: you just happen to be in the way when the child wants to test limits. If you can remain firm, not overly blaming, and keep your sense of humor operating, your child will in all likelihood emerge very well from the four-year-old "hyper" stage and move into the five-year-old "Mommy's helper" stage (only to set you up so he can let you down again as he moves toward six, another age of violent extremes).

Between four and five the child is steadily moving out of a self-centered world and beginning to find his place among his peers. This is not an easy time for him. In addition to the testing-the-limits impulses which arise from within, he must face the ever-increasing challenge of discovering a way to relate to what is external: he must face the challenge of competition. Although the urge to compete does not become a real focal point until from about six on, it is felt strongly before then.

Our discussion of the four- and five-year-old child will begin with another area, however, that of the development of learning skills. The more we carry out and understand psychoeducational research, the more we view the preschool years as important. Four is an age at which it can be told, in many instances, whether or not the child is developing appropriate preacademic skills (social and emotional, language, sensory-motor coordination, background of experience) and hence is an age at which remedial or insurance steps can be taken should they be needed. So the wise parent will be on the alert for any problems or potential problems in learning, any weakness in the preschool skills. Recognition will be easier and more reliable during the four-to-five age span than earlier, both because many of the problems noted earlier will have disappeared (not having been real problems), and because others, present before only in bud form, will appear in bolder relief.

PROBLEMS IN LEARNING

There are many reasons why a child might not learn efficiently. He may have some physical disability, like blindness or deafness. He may suffer some major or minor lesion of the central nervous system. One or more of his perceptual-motor circuits may not operate with efficiency. He may be so overburdened with emotional problems that he cannot apply the skills he has acquired.

But in our discussion we will limit attention to those children who fall into the category of *underachiever*. An underachiever is a child whose day-by-day efficiency is markedly lower than one would expect on the basis of his intelligence. He is not mentally retarded: he does not lack intellectual power. Nor is he physically disabled, as is the blind or the deaf child.

There are three major causes for a learning problem: (1) cultural deprivation, a lack of proper stimulation in the early years, which results in an attitude antithetical to "academic" learning; (2) bio-neuro-psychological difficulties—those caused by the *simultaneous* interaction of physical, neurological, and psychological forces that interfere with the ability to learn in a regular class setting, for example, inherent irritability, deficient attention span, inadequate eye-hand coordination, constant confusion between right and left, up and down, an inability to maintain logical reasoning categories; (3) emotional inhibitions, which interfere with the capacities vital for the learning process, for example, attention and recall. Any underachiever can be shown to be suffering difficulties in one or more of these categories.

Obviously, if you try to increase your child's background of cultural experiences, attend to difficulties in his physical, neurological, and psychological make-up, and avoid piling him high with inhibitions, you will be faced with an incredibly tall order. But there *are* things you can do to help your young child learn.

BACKGROUND OF EXPERIENCE

It is not enough to expose a child to a wide banquet table of choices, though this is what so many parents do. Mere exposure accomplishes little by itself. Endless trips to museums and art galleries produce few results if there is no preparation for them. The trick is to make the material *meaningful* to the child.

We recall taking our first son to the zoo and pointing out the hippopotamus as something worthy of his awe and attention. He looked over toward the hippo. But by his comments and questions we realized that what he was paying attention to was a common, garden-variety pigeon sitting near the hippo. He had had experience with pigeons, but none with hippos. So a relatively bright child can overlook even a hippopotamus (which is not easy to overlook) if he lacks meaningful preparation.

How many parents insist that their child take time-consuming, expensive music lessons only to discover that the child sustains no real interest in music? How many parents insist their children attend religious school only to find that no real convictions are formed? In both situations much of the trouble can be explained by the fact that the children's studies were mere oases in deserts of disinterest. Music lessons in a nonmusical, noninterested family? Religious instruction in a family lacking religious conviction? Although an occasionally bright, motivated child may profit from cases of exposure, he is an exception.

Here are some devices that may help make exposures meaningful to your child.

1. Prepare for an event by discussing it beforehand. What does the child already know? What is he interested in? What will he seek to observe, to find out? What questions will he ask himself?

2. Encourage him to think about the event as it takes place, by showing some interest in what *he* has to say. Don't *you* spout off. Listen to him. This will foster independence in addition to interest.

3. Engage in follow-up activities after the exposure. What did the child learn? What surprised him—what did he not think was so? What new questions does he have, questions to which he can seek answers the next time?

SPECIFIC SKILLS

There are many exercises and games that can help a child develop skills essential for effective learning. The home, the street, the backyard, the supermarket can all be sites of preschool learning— learning that should be fun. For example, when a child looks at and identifies certain packages in a supermarket, he is developing visual discrimination skills. His mother should encourage this type of activity as a game, as fun, and not with the words "Now we are having a lesson in visual discrimination."

With that in mind, let's list some of these activities.

1. To help the child develop smooth control of his body and its parts, particularly the different muscle groups, have the child work on so-called large-muscle skills by throwing and catching a ball, learning to balance, jumping, and skipping, and encourage small muscle (and other coordinative) activities by letting him reach for things successfully, cut with scissors, hold and use a

pencil, turn pages, and button clothes. Nonanxious, nonpushy encouragement is what the child needs in these areas. Foundation skill 3, encouraging independence, is excruciatingly important here. The mother who robs a child of his independence by dressing him when he could dress himself is doing him the additional disservice of depriving him of opportunities to sharpen his perceptual-motor skills.

2. To help the child learn to distinguish different spoken sounds when he hears them—a differentiation that provides one of the important bases for language development—speak carefully and play rhyming games with him. Play games in which you ask the child to tell if you are saying the same word twice or two different words. Ask him to tell you words that sound like words you tell him. Help him to stretch out the number of sounds he can listen to and differentiate by telling him interesting stories.

3. To help develop visual discrimination—the ability to differentiate information presented by the eyes to the brain—show the child pictures with parts missing and ask what's missing. Show the child pictures of things that are nearly alike but not quite and ask him to point out what is different. Play games like Old Maid which encourage the search for visual similarities. Encourage him to help you with pictures and labels in the supermarket. Then move gradually to simple words.

4. Encourage the child to develop skills in directionality. Play a game like Simon Says and include in it calls for him to wiggle his left foot or lift his right arm—and then ask him to point to the left or right side of others. From this move off to differences in direction in relation to objects, to rooms, and to pages in a comic book. Show him how the movement is from left to right. If you have a little girl, encourage her to set the table, paying attention to appropriate left-right placement of forks and spoons.

SOCIAL AND EMOTIONAL FACTORS

Nowhere will the child's independence or lack thereof show itself so readily as in relation to his initial experience with school. Here are some of the things he must be helped with if he is to have a successful school experience:

1. He needs practice in separating from his mother and **should** have it often before it is time for him to attend school.
2. He must learn to relate to and share adults other than his parents frequently.
3. He must be taught all the many skills that will make him feel self-reliant and in control of himself at school: how to dress and undress himself, how to recognize his own clothing, how to wash himself, how to manage himself at the toilet, how to keep track of his papers and his lunch box.
4. At the same time, he should have the confidence to ask for help when he cannot master some need for himself, for example, to ask where the bathroom is when he is unaccustomed to a building.
5. He should have a fairly well-developed notion of sharing, and respect for the rights and properties of others.

CHECKING FOR POTENTIAL LEARNING PROBLEMS

The following checklist may help you to recognize potential learning problems—deficiencies in essential skills—in your child. Don't let the list alarm you. If your child fits one of the descriptions on the list, that does not mean he definitely has a learning problem. What it does mean is that a closer look is needed—perhaps a trip to his physician or a psychoeducational evaluation. Remember, it is much easier to treat both learning problems and potential learning problems if you detect them early. Psychoeducational evaluations may be expensive, but when you realize that you are dealing with at least twelve years of your child's life (his minimum time in school), you will see why we think it may be a good investment.

1. Most children communicate fairly well by the age of three, the majority a good many months before that time. If your child is still having significant difficulty in making himself understood, ask your physician to recommend an evaluation.

2. How is your child's large-muscle coordination? How well does he walk, run, jump, throw a ball? Is he fairly well coordinated or does he seem unduly clumsy? We certainly are not implying that every clumsy child will have a learning problem. But large-muscle clumsiness *may* be a sign of future difficulty and, at any rate, is worth a psychoeducational evaluation.

3. How is your child's small-muscle coordination? How well does he tie his shoes, use scissors, paper, and pencil?

4. Does your five-year-old show persistent confusion and inconsistency about right and left? We are not concerned whether he eats with his right hand but kicks with his left foot. What is important is this: Does he show no clear right-left preference, and does he seem confused and awkward when playing a game like Simon Says?

5. Does your five-year-old seem able to maintain certain logical categories of thought? Or is he likely to offer the following as a sensible list: Summer, winter, Tuesday, Christmas? Children with conceptual problems are likely to offer that kind of list when asked to name the four seasons.

6. Is your child too nervous to sit still and pay attention? Is he never, for example, able to listen to an interesting story?

7. How are his vision and hearing?

8. Are you giving your child experience, cultural and otherwise, in terms of which future experiences can be evaluated and understood?

9. Do you live in a neighborhood that devalues education—

where the child who cares about school is labeled "oddball"? If you do, you deal with a tough problem. The real remedy involves mass community action. It cannot be solved at the level of one family alone. (See our book *Bright Child—Poor Grades* for a discussion of this issue.)

10. Does your child show the appropriate degree of independence for a child about to start school? Can he separate from you?

These are some of the questions to ask yourself as you wonder whether your child is ready for a learning experience. Some school systems evaluate each child before school starts, but many of these evaluations are superficial.

Be especially wary of anyone who tells you your child is "immature" without explaining what is meant by the term. This label has become a vast wastebasket into which are thrown children of all types. All the term should mean is that the child is engaging in behavior typical of younger children. But is it the type of behavior that will clear up with the mere passage of time? If the child is really immature the implication is that the behavior was normal at some age, and the child is merely developing slowly. But all too often the term is used in conjunction with conditions that the child is unlikely to grow out of without special help. There are serious language problems and highly neurotic patterns of extreme inhibition or excessive aggressiveness that have been labeled immature. These patterns are not normal at any age and cannot be ended without special help.

Should someone label your child immature, ask him to explain both what he means, and what, if anything, can be done about it. If he says the mere passage of time will help, fine. But if he speaks of a learning problem, or a significant neurosis, think in terms of remedies. Labels are of no use unless they lead to informed action. Waiting can be a legitimate action, if based on the knowledge that it is the best available alternative.

IMAGINARY COMPANIONS

During the late three's and early four's (and on rare occasions later still), it is not unusual for a child to shock his parents by speaking of an imaginary companion as though it were real. The parents suspect the child knows the companion isn't real, but they're not sure—and they cannot get an outright statement from the child.

This situation is best handled by foundation skill 4, an acknowledgment: "You would like it if your little friend were real, but we both know that this is a game." It is wasted energy to get upset. In almost all cases, unless something else is rather seriously the matter, the child will give up the companion in due time.

However, should the "game" continue longer than one year, it might be wise to seek a professional evaluation. And should the child give a persistent impression that he thinks the friend is really real, professional help might be sought sooner.

"STEALING"

This is one of the bum raps handed to too many children. Very young children, even those four and five years old, have not yet consolidated an adult version of ownership. So the young child who appropriates things for himself is not to be thought of as a thief. True, he should be stopped, and things explained to him. But he should not be labeled a thief, for as we have pointed out before, children have a perverse way of living up to their labels.

The child who *persistently* takes things not belonging to him does need close attention. There is no single reason why a child does this. He may take things because he feels deprived in other areas. He may seek revenge on his parents. But whatever his reason, the problem is best approached by trying to do something about the cause of the behavior. Meanwhile, the behavior itself should be stopped by applying the proper limits and by using foundation skill 4, reflecting to the child that he seems happy or satisfied only when he can appropriate something belonging to someone else.

Many parents seek deliberately to trap their children by leaving desirable things lying about. This is stupid (and mean).

Another big mistake parents make is in attempting to force their child to confess his crime. When he doesn't, they become furious. This is a waste of time. Even adult criminals are not forced to testify against themselves. After one has seen the punishment some parents hand out, it is not hard to understand why children do not want to incriminate themselves. The parents will shout, "We know you did it! Why did you do it?" And the child will not answer. If the truth were to be known, the child *cannot* answer because he probably does not really know why he took the article in question.

If you are sure your child took some money, proceed with the limit and the acknowledgment. Spare yourself and your child the ordeal of confession. You might say, "The money will have to be replaced from your allowance. I guess you're not happy unless you feel you're taking something that isn't yours."

In extreme or chronic cases, seek professional help. Genuine psychopathic behavior, that is, faulty behavior based on the deepset conviction that stealing is the best way to get things is hard to change.

"LYING"

This is another area where parents create nightmares. Telling the truth is not an inherent trait. People not only tend to see things from their own points of view, and from emotional rather than intellectual perspectives, but they are motivated by the instinct for self-preservation. If you are a harsh, punishing, rejecting person, and you expect your children to tell the truth, you are in for a rude shock. Even children with rather mild-mannered parents do not always tell the adult version of the truth.

Telling the truth *is* apparently much easier for the very young child. But as the child gets older he becomes somewhat doubtful of the glories of truth-telling, especially if his parents rely heavily on blame as a control device. If he proceeds in a rather normal fashion, he will come back to the idea of telling the truth, as he develops enough personality strength to admit his mistakes—develops a personality in which errors are not seen as catastrophic—and as he becomes convinced that truth-telling is much easier in the long run than telling lies.

Some parents make a fetish of telling the truth: "I'll teach you to lie, damn you!" These same parents often make a fetish of respect: "I'll teach that kid to have respect!" What they fail to realize in both cases is that telling the truth and parental respect are by-products of an otherwise healthy life. They cannot be taught directly by the law of the lash. You can force a child to say "Sir" by beating him, but only until he gets strong enough to fight back.

So too with truth-telling. You cannot command a child to tell the truth. First of all, you are not always in a position to judge whether the child's version of some event is truthful. Secondly, you are not always going to be around with your lash when the truth is needed from your child.

It is far better to let truth-telling—and respect—develop naturally, as you try your best to be what you consider an otherwise good parent.

Suppose you walk into a room and the circumstantial evidence is overwhelming that the child committed some deed. You ask him whether he did it. He says no, he didn't. At this point, some parents would scream, "We know you did it, so stop lying to us. That's why we're mad. If you told the truth, we wouldn't be so angry." And they would get nowhere.

Instead, if it is really something important, and some limit need be applied, proceed with the limit. "I'm sorry, Jimmy. I think you did do it, and this is something we absolutely cannot permit."

REFUSING TO EAT

A child's eating patterns vary from age to age. The nonanxious mother will be prepared to cope with this natural variability, but the overly concerned mother may panic and start a problem where none existed.

Sometimes a child discovers he can blackmail his parents by refusing to eat. Should a parent fall for this gambit, she'd better be prepared to lose every serious argument that comes along. For once a child discovers an area in which a parent can be blackmailed, watch out.

If your child refuses food in order to win some point, do not back down. Let him miss the meal. If you are terribly concerned, check first with his physician. But in the absence of a serious medical condition, it is far better to allow the child to miss the meal than to hand over to him a way of blackmailing you.

INFANTILE TOILET BEHAVIOR

Somewhere between the ages of four and five it is not unusual for a child to revert suddenly to infantile toilet patterns. This is especially likely to occur with the birth of a new sibling.

Don't panic.

Remember skills 1 and 4. Stay nonblaming, and acknowledge the child's feelings: "Sometimes it's fun to want to go back and live like a baby, but I think you'll find that it's even more fun to have the advantages that go with growing up." Make him responsible for his own cleanup (as much as is possible for his age).

Do the same with bed-wetting. Bed-wetting is a behavioral act with no clear implications. Some bed-wetting children suffer serious emotional conflicts, while others seem essentially normal in every way. Stay nonblaming, encourage independence, acknowledge the embarrassment, and forget about it—after a medical check. Make the child responsible for changing sheets. Do not get up in the middle of the night to change bedding.

Sometimes the anti-wetting devices work; often they don't. Some introduce more problems than they solve. Any device which ensnares the parents in the child's difficulties by making them responsible for waking the child repeatedly may do more harm than good: the parents may find themselves trading bed-wetting for a more seriously entrenched dependency pattern.

FEAR OF THE DARK

Fear of the dark is common at all ages and comes in a variety of intensities and durations. It is, in and of itself, not a reliable indication of the child's overall adjustment. Sometimes it is encountered in undisturbed children and at other times in rather seriously disturbed children.

There are a number of things you can do to help the child who fears the dark—many of them the same as for children with other fears. First of all, do not pooh-pooh the fear nor call it silly. Acknowledge that you realize the child has the fear and add that he will not always feel that way: "I realize you're afraid of the dark, Jimmy, and that it upsets you to be alone in the dark. I also realize you won't always feel that way."

Sometimes fears are part of the fallout of some recent trauma the child has faced. When this is so, deal directly with the traumatic basis of the fear, even though the child does not see the connection:

"Jimmy, I know you feel very sorry that Mitchell just moved away. Perhaps you feel you won't be able to make new friends. I think that may have something to do with your new fear of the dark."

"What are you talking about, Mom? That has nothing to do with it. I'm just scared to stay by myself in the dark."

"Yes, I know you are. I also know you won't feel that way all the time."

As you can see, no big point is made about the child's refusal to accept the suggested relationship between the fear of making new friends, the sadness at losing an old one, and the recent fear of the darkness. Nevertheless, our experience has indicated that if the suggestion is valid, it will help.

There is another system to consider for ending your child's fear of the dark: direct habit retraining. This is the technique we used with the younger child afraid of the bath: the technique by which the child is helped to come to grips with his fear by being exposed to it in gradually increased dosages. There is no universal agreement on why this technique is effective—or on whether it is anything more than plain old-fashioned suggestion. But in our opinion, habit retraining does indeed help *some* children in *some* instances and has a legitimate place in the total methodology of changing behavior. Let's see how it could be applied to a fear of the dark.

1. Write down a list of situations in which the circumstances most feared are at one end of the scale, and those in which the child is most relaxed and comfortable at the other. Let the child help with the list as much as he can. On one end of the scale might be a situation in which the child lies in his bed, alone, in a totally dark room. At the other end might be the child lying in front of the TV, with the entire family present.

2. Develop step by step a set of situations, working from both ends toward the middle. If lying alone at night in a darkened room with the door closed is the very worst situation for the child, the next worst might be alone in the room with the door open. Next might be alone in the room with the door open and some adult in an adjoining room. And so forth. Working from the other end, the next best situation to being with the family in front of the TV, might be being in front of the TV

with others home but in different rooms. The next step might be in front of the TV with no one home. Try to develop at least twelve situations, with the most feared at one end, and the most comfortable at the other.

3. Ask your child to lean back, close his eyes, and get a picture in his mind of the most comfortable situation. Ask him to explain to you, as best he can, how he feels. He will probably experience little or no anxiety when visualizing the most comfortable situation, so proceed to the next step. Go one step at a time until he tells you that he feels more anxious. (*Explain to him that you are not interested in how anxious he imagines he would be in the various pictured situations, but how anxious he is at the time you are carrying out the procedure.* In other words, ask him, "How do you feel—*right now?*") When the anxiety level goes up, go back to the preceding step. If even this step now makes him feel anxious (because he is still feeling the tension of the preceding step) go back still another, and yet another step—if need be. When the anxiety level drops to what it was at the beginning of the series, proceed in a forward direction from wherever you happen now to be.

4. You will find it helpful to encourage the child to relax his muscles during each of the steps (see Chapter 4).

5. If you decide to use actual situations instead of images, either because the child is too young to follow the instructions, or because it is easy to duplicate the real life situation, work with a much shorter list. Explain to the child that you know he is afraid of the dark, that you also know he will not always feel that way, and that you are going to have him act out step by step a method that will help him regain confidence in himself. Each step means that he goes to bed under a different set of circumstances. Tell the child what all the steps will be in advance, but *do not try to skip a step even if the child thinks he wants to speed things up.* He may speed things up for the moment, but the overall effectiveness may be lost.

The total sequence might go like this.

First night: Lights on, door open, radio on. The child stays in his room for fifteen minutes under these conditions relaxing. He is allowed to fall asleep with the lights on and the door open.

Second night: Lights on, door open, radio off. After fifteen minutes, the door is partially closed, but the lights stay on. The child is allowed to fall asleep this way.

Third night: Lights on, door open. This time the door is partially closed after five minutes. Asleep with lights on.

Fourth night: Lights on, door open. After fifteen minutes the light goes off, the door remains partially open.

From here on in, the steps would be gauged by what the child agrees would be adequate steps.

16

From Age Six to Eight

Young six is a creature of extremes, but he remains enthusiastic and anxious to learn. He has two large obstacles looming in front of him in the external world: peers—anxious to enter into competition with him; and school—possibly lurking to do him in.

Although the six-year-old is eager to learn, he can be very dogmatic—especially (in fact, almost exclusively) at home. His parents may think it is amazing that he listens to the teacher, since he certainly does not seem interested in listening to them. He still needs to solve his dependency relations with his parents. He wants to be independent of them and at the same time knows he needs them. Hence the stormy, dogmatic behavior.

Seven is not a good year, and hence second grade is not always a pleasant experience. Children who had no trouble in first grade may seem unhappy in second. The seven-year-old has a lot of self-doubts and broods quite a bit. He often rejects limits, and complains a lot.

As the child moves from seven to eight he goes through a period in which he is often unrealistic about his own capacities, as he both over- and under-estimates himself. Most eight-year-olds we have known have been happy and productive, but have a marked flair for the dramatic: "You hate me! I know you do!"

THE ABILITY TO BE COMPETITIVE

The ability to be competitive is exceedingly important, if by competition we mean pursuing appropriate self-interested goals. By competitive we do *not* mean a tendency to be aggressive for its own sake, or to strike out at imagined obstacles.

Appropriate competitiveness is a by-product of an otherwise healthy personality: healthy competitiveness cannot be bred per se (as can hostile competitiveness). All the foundation skills have to be used in its development. If parents are overly blaming, the child will think of himself as unworthy and be an ineffectual competitor. Or he will develop an intense fear of failure, feeling his entire sense of self-worth rides on everything attempted. Since he cannot win or be successful all the time, he may thereby retreat from *all* competitive situations.

If the child has not been encouraged to be independent, he will feel himself in need of continued praise and love from others and so will fear competition, believing it might make someone else angry. A dependent child cannot be a nonanxious competitor. The only way he can compete is at great psychological expense. The dependent child also fears new things.

A mother who has not set appropriate limits or who has smothered her child is likely to have an anxious child. An anxious child, or a spoiled child, cannot be competitive. They are plagued by contradictory emotions when they attempt to behave in a consistently competitive manner.

Parents who try to live through their children—who force their children to be carriers of parental ambitions—take big risks. Some few children tolerate this type of pressure very well, but for the majority such pressure complicates everything. Should the child perceive his parents are interested in him only to the extent that he can achieve, he is likely to confuse his feelings for himself as an entire person with his attitudes toward accomplishment. A single loss, inevitable in any endeavor, will be experienced as a catastrophic loss of total self-esteem. A person who must operate under this type of condition often ceases operating altogether under the theory that it is better not to try anything at all than to try something that may be failed. Such is the genesis of a widespread form of underachievement. (See "The Psychology of Underachievement" in our book *Bright Child—Poor Grades*.)

A fear of appropriate competition comes in many guises. The child may fail in school. He may refuse to play competitive sport games. He may find himself the continuing butt of jokes. He may develop assorted aches and pains and cling to his parents.

It is not easy to set up a remedial program for the child who fears competition, because diagnosis is not easy—especially in the absence of psychological testing. There are many things that can cause a fear of competition. Furthermore, there are other conditions which resemble a fear of competitiveness but are something else: a child who patterns himself after a passive adult may appear inhibited and fearful of competition on the surface but actually merely lack a model for hard work and discipline.

Nevertheless, there are a number of things parents can do to help the noncompetitive child, regardless of the cause of his problem.

1. Follow all of the foundation skills, with special attention to skills 1 and 3, remaining nonblaming and encouraging independence.
2. Show a healthy, appropriate, straightforward interest in his achievement, but do not mix up your feelings for *him* with your attitudes toward his *accomplishments*. This will help him to keep an appropriate perspective, avoid developing an intense fear of failure, and avoid linking a particular success or lack of success with his entire sense of worth as a person.

   One way parents can keep a proper perspective is, as we have seen, to remain in a "content"- rather than an "evaluation"-oriented mood when talking about schoolwork. Show more interest in *what* your child is learning than how well. What with report cards, teachers and other children's comments, the child gets more than his fill of evaluation anyway. Should a child show you a project on the space program, why not comment on the space program? This is easy, and it accomplishes a lot. For one thing, it shows the child you are genuinely interested in learning. At the same time, it points the way for him: it shows him that he ought to think about what he is learning and not be consumed with worry about how well he is doing.

Unfortunately, the typical parent rarely concentrates on the content of schoolwork.

"Look at this chart, Daddy. It shows the stages of a rocket."

"Hmm. That isn't drawn too neatly. And I think you left a stage out."

That is an obviously negative approach. But here is another version, which seems positive and yet perpetuates the same faulty belief—that the evaluative aspect of a piece of work is all anyone should be concerned with.

"Look at this chart, Daddy. It shows the stages of a rocket."

"Very well done, son. I see you got an "A" for that."

We do not mean parents should not teach their children. But this is not the time for it. Teaching is done by example —your *own* interest in your own achievement—and at appropriate times.

3. Provide an adequate model for the child. Show him you value competitive achievement—for yourself.

4. Deal with his fears directly. Suppose your child does poorly at some sports competition. The typical father is no help at all to his boy in such a situation: "What's the matter with you? You damn sissy!" or "Get out there and punch him back."

This not only fails to help the child, but makes him worse.

Instead, remember skills 1 and 4, remain nonblaming, and acknowledge his fear. When the child realizes you do not denounce him for his fears, his own stock in himself will go up. This is a good first step toward developing the kind of confidence needed to be an appropriately aggressive competitor. Acknowledge his fears directly: "I realize you feel upset. You want to do better, but it's still hard for you. Perhaps you won't always feel that way. Perhaps you will. It doesn't really matter." (Of course, these words must be said honestly. If you cannot see the truth or value of this particular approach, by no means use it.)

With children who seem desperately afraid of being hurt, you might add, "Right now you're still very worried about getting hurt." Believe it or not, this simple acknowledgment will help reduce the fear. It may not conquer it completely —that depends on many factors, not all of which are reachable by parents—but it will help. If your child is not worried so much about getting hurt as he is about *doing* the hurting, say, "Right now it still upsets you to hurt someone else even if they have hurt you first." Very often both fears, of hurting and of being hurt, go together. Both acknowledging statements can be used together.

5. Should the fears persist, seek professional help. This is not an area to ignore.

THE CHILD WHO DOES NOT DO HIS HOMEWORK

Homework has many purposes: to review what has already been covered and hence discover areas of weakness; to consolidate what has already been covered; to go over new work not yet covered; to commit to memory those things learned by drill. But there is one overriding purpose of homework that exceeds all of the others in importance: it helps the child to learn to work independently, without adult help. (For this reason, we are against school programs that force parents to work repeatedly with their children on homework assignments: parental help should be confined to times when the child is really stuck.)

If your child is not doing his homework, your first step is to find out why. Is the work over his head? Does he need tutoring? Is he in the right grade? Does he have the appropriate background skills?

Or, is it that he *can* do it but just chooses not to? He either puts it off or does it so hurriedly that it makes no sense. This is the child we are interested in at this point.

To help him:

1. Use the family council to get him to set up a plan. If and when he does not follow his own plan, inform him he will have to design another. Get the other children at the council to discuss homework—its purpose, and the way they do it. Try to put it in perspective, and point out its values.

2. Interpret the child's lack of independence: "Michael, you're waiting for us to make you do it. We don't want that job."

3. After the child has shown he can understand and accept that interpretation, interpret his fear of growing up and assuming responsibilities more directly. "Michael, there's a part of all of us that wants to remain a child. Believe it or not that part actually wants someone else to give orders—to take over, as a parent would for a child. That's the part of you that actually wants us to be responsible for your schoolwork, and to tell you what to do. But we'd like you to do the job on your own."

4. Continue using the council and these acknowledgments and reflections as long as is necessary. If the child resists all attempts at helping him to become more independent, seek professional help. The ability to function independently is too important to leave to chance. Remember to use all of the information in Chapter 8.

SIBLING BICKERING

A certain amount of sibling bickering is normal in the sense that all siblings do it, and there is as yet no way to stamp it out.

It has many bases: jealousy, a fear of being cheated of scarce resources, and a need for negative attention.

Aside from treating the suspected underlying causes—reducing the need for negative attention, acknowledging the inevitable jealousies—parents ought to arm themselves with a few simple rules, brought up and discussed at the family council.

If one particular child has a need to tease his siblings unmercifully, pay special attention to all that was said on the need for negative attention. Additionally, interpret his needs directly: "Joseph, the only time you seem able to feel good about yourself is when you put someone else down. I guess that sort of thing is still very important to you. I hope it doesn't last too long." If this can be said frequently enough, out of earshot of others in front of whom the child would feel embarrassed, and *if it is said non-blamingly as a pure and simple statement of fact*, it might be listened to—eventually.

FEAR OF ILLNESS AND DEATH

These fears should be considered problematic only if they persist a long time after they cease to be appropriate. A child might mourn a very close relative (a parent or sibling) as long as a year, though *intensely* sad emotions should taper off before that.

Should a child's fear of illness or death persist a long time, it is likely we are dealing either with some form of neurosis or with a situation in which the child is consciously or unconsciously gaining something from continuing to mourn: sympathy, attention, or license to discontinue some task that was difficult for him.

Should your child's fears of death and/or illness continue, consider the following:

1. Has he been given an adequate chance to air his feelings? Children should not be forced to talk about something they do not want to talk about, but the door should be left open.
2. Is he gaining something from his protracted brooding? If so, interpret it to him: "Johnny—it seems that when you get sad what you're really trying to tell us is that you're afraid to go back to school where you were having such trouble with math."

3. Children usually equate death with loneliness. Assure them they will be with you for a very long time.

4. Children feel also that what happened to someone else may happen to them or to you. Assure them this is unlikely. Remember: children rarely complain directly about what is really bothering them in this area. Their fears may appear to be genuine concern for the dead person, but this is rare in children.

FEAR OF GOING TO SCHOOL

When a child will not go to school, it may be because he fears the school and/or fears to separate from his parents. In most cases, it is wise to get the child back in school as soon as possible. In intense cases, where professional help is required, the therapist can judge the proper time to push the child toward school, but this is an educated guess at best. Sometimes the decision must be reevaluated.

The most frequent cause of the school fear is separation anxiety —a fear of leaving the parents. This kind of basic fear manifests itself differently at different ages and can go underground during some periods. So the fact that a child was able to separate from his parents before does not preclude the possibility that separation anxiety may be causing his problems now. A lack of independence in a very young child may show up as crying, whining, nagging; this same lack of independence may show up at a later age as a refusal to dress. At still later ages, the lack of independence and concomitant separation anxiety may show up as a refusal to do homework, or go to school.

The following suggestions may be helpful if your child will not go to school.

1. Stay nonblaming. You will have a strong tendency to get very angry with him, not only because you are worried about the

school he is missing, but because you blame yourself for not helping him. Parents often attempt to deal with their own sorrow by trying to force the child back to school—as though they were sweeping him under the rug. If they don't have to see the child walking around the house when he should be in school, they don't feel so sorrowful and guilty.

You will also be angry because you half suspect the child is faking. He says he's in agony in the morning: his stomach hurts—everything hurts. But somehow as soon as you give him permission to stay home he feels all better. Yet the child is not faking: he really is scared and believes he must stay home.

2. Acknowledge his fears while you exert strong pressure to get him to attend. You must remain adamant about his need to continue attending school and at the same time let him know you realize he feels afraid. "I realize you feel afraid—that you're not lying. At the same time I realize it would not help you to let you stay home. In fact you would lose even more confidence in yourself. I have to insist you go to school."

3. If the child falls to the ground, screams, and holds your legs, and continues this kind of behavior for at least 3 days, seek professional help.

BODY MANIFESTATIONS OF TENSION

Whether the child develops a definite symptom like a facial tic, a rash or a stomach ache or just *thinks* he has some body disorder, begin his treatment program with a trip to the physician. It is wise to do this in every case that involves a body manifestation, and it is essential where pain, including headaches, is concerned. Not only can the physician help rule out physical disease, but he can give meaningful reassurance to the child.

Body manifestations of psychological tensions should always be evaluated by a professional psychotherapist as well as a physician. The therapist is in a position to judge whether the case can be treated at home or whether additional professional help is needed.

There are certain things that can be done on the home front: stay nonblaming, do not pooh-pooh the pain, and yet make sure the child does not get extra favors—like ice cream or parental overconcern.

THE OBSESSIVE-COMPULSIVE CHILD

Children who brood excessively or who perform some ritualistic act with high frequency—wash their hands, repeat certain phrases —need professional handling.

The parents of an obsessional child may have fallen down on foundation skill 3, the encouragement of independence, and have made the child frightened of aggressiveness. Shore up the structure along the lines spelled out in chapter 8. Again, be sympathetic to the child, but rocklike in your refusal to allow him to gain anything from his symptoms.

17

From Age Nine to Twelve

These are the years that seem harder for girls than for boys. The girls' moods swing more strongly: the ups are uppier, the downs downier, and the secretiveness greater.

The nine-year-old has great vitality, likes to be with his friends, wants less and less to be with his family (except to announce "There's nothing to do around here!"), and is frequently boastful: "Do that once more, and I'll flatten you." Like the eight-year-old he maintains a sense of the dramatic and can make a stuffy nose sound like a true medical emergency: "The nose drops! Quick, the drops!"

Ten is known as a stable and happy age, but the eleven-year-old goes the "hyper" path again. Twelve is hard to predict; there are wide variations, and generalizations seem more difficult as youngsters move from the child stage to puberty.

Age thirteen is secretive. We have seen thirteen-year-old girls with serious problems who could not bring themselves to admit those problems: "Everything is fine—really."

THE FOURTH-GRADE PROBLEM

The material is much harder in fourth grade than it was in third, as more and more content is offered.

It is not infrequent that learning problems, actually present since the beginning, are demonstrated at this time—pushed out into the open by the more demanding work.

Skill 4, acknowledgments, will help: "I can understand how upsetting things are now. The work is harder; you wonder if you'll be able to do it. And sometimes it's hard to decide whether to study or play all the time."

HOW MUCH TV? MOVIES?

How much should a child be allowed to watch TV?

How often should he go to the movies?

How much of his money should he be allowed to spend on his hobbies and how much time should he be able to devote to them?

We are frequently asked such questions by parents who apparently feel there is some correct amount of time children should be allowed for these pastimes. Indeed there is a correct amount —but it is correct only for one particular child. What is a proper amount of time for one child may be too much or too little for another.

The amount of time a child should be allowed to engage in these activities has nothing to do with the activity itself but rather with how well the child is taking care of the necessities in his life—his health, chores, and schoolwork. If these are taken care of, the rest of the time is his.

The family council, as we have seen, is a good place to review these issues.

Suppose your child feels he should watch endless amounts of TV. Instead of trying to determine arbitrarily how much TV is too much TV, ask yourself, "How well is he handling his responsibilities?" If these are taken care of, then it is safe to give him a free hand in making his own decisions. After all, the thing you are worried about is that the pastimes will cut down the time he should be spending on other, more important endeavors. So let the rest of his life be your guide. It is difficult to generalize about TV. We try to soft-pedal it in our family to leave more time for intellectually active pursuits like reading and drawing. But we do not make a big fuss over the issue. If we chose to, we would use the family council.

Some children are so deficient in peer skills or so unable to assume active and assertive attitudes that TV is all they have. We have worked with some of these children and have listened to their parents complain: "All the kid does is sit in front of the damn television set." And while we sympathized with the parents' feelings, inwardly we were grateful for the TV, for without it some of these ego-deficient children would have nothing. Nevertheless, such children are rare.

"I HAVE NOTHING TO DO"

This is not the first age at which the complaint is heard. And many a mother, falling right into the trap, accepts the charge implicit in the complaint. She assumes that (a) it is her fault the child can find nothing to do, and (b) it is her job to set things straight; she is the child's social director.

In some cases, it *is* the mother's fault the child has nothing to do. These are the cases in which the mother fell down on foundation skill 3 and did not grant appropriate independence. She wanted to control her child's life. He fought her initially. Then he became addicted to her overmanipulative ways. Now he not only gives in to her demands, but has gotten to *like* the idea of being controlled. And so from resisting her suggestions, he now seeks them—in fact, *demands* them.

Use skills 1, 3, and 4 with the child who demands you find him something to do. Stay nonblaming. Encourage independence. Acknowledge his upset: "You somehow feel it's my job to find you something to do and it upsets you when I don't."

"It *is* your job," the child will shout.

This is when to give a sympathetic grunt and retire from the conversation. Do not argue back and do not give in. The child will gradually get the idea.

GANG ATTACKS

Sometimes a gang of children will make one child the butt of all their teasing and aggression—often one not adept at defending himself.

We use the following rule of thumb to determine when adults should intervene: if many children are physically attacking one child, adult intervention is warranted. It's fine to let a child fight his own battles—but not against unfair odds. We have the police to protect us from unfair odds. Children ought to have the same protection.

If the bully is one child, or if the aggression is merely verbal, another approach is probably better: to find out in what way the child stimulates the aggression. Some children not only stimulate it but actually *invite* it.

Remember: you cannot run ahead of your child and smooth the path of life for him, no matter how strong the temptation might be. You must reduce his vulnerabilities so he can face whatever life will throw at him.

There is one rather sure way of protecting a child from being made the butt of jokes and from being bullied: help him develop talents and competencies.

Make sure a boy is not overprotected. Let him learn to be good at sports. Give him swimming lessons. Encourage him to watch and learn from older children. But do this in a relaxed manner. Should he remain passive, follow the suggestions given for the noncompetitive person.

Find out how the child is stimulating the jibes. Does he walk or talk oddly? Does he brag too much (the most frequent cause for other children ganging up)? Do you force him to dress in some completely ridiculous adult style, inappropriate to his peer group?

18

From Age Thirteen to Fifteen

One child may be mature from a social and/or psychosexual standpoint at age thirteen or fourteen, while another may not mature until he is fifteen or sixteen. Some children in the early teens develop a strong interest in the opposite sex while other children have either moderate interest or none at all. A good many children lose interest in school—some permanently. Some children show a continuing ability to accept authority while others are hard put to keep even a semblance of respect.

The teen years are years of searching and researching, of deciding which attitudes to keep and which to discard, of deciding how finally to relate to people. In short, these are the years in which youth must find a home among men—a way to live, to work, to love, and to be productive. (See the writings of Erik Erikson for insightful accounts of the interrelations between biological heritage, psychological equipment, and the roles of society.)

A great deal of work goes on during the teen years. We wince when parents get angry and disgusted at their teen-age children for lying around their bedrooms: "Why don't they do something? They're so damn lazy!" If those parents could only realize all the work going on inwardly.

The parent has many jobs to perform during his offspring's adolescence: to be a sounding board against which the teen-ager can test (or hurl) his ideas; to be a needler—good-naturedly and not sarcastically—of *some* of the child-adult's ideas; to provide a relatively coherent code of life from which the child can draw in times of trouble and push against during those moments when he is searching for his own identity; to provide a nonblaming, non-condemning voice of reason; and to provide a quiet, nonpushy, nonobvious source of love and affection.

Channels of communication range from poor to nonexistent between teen-agers and adults; our first job is to offer some ways of keeping these channels at least partly open.

COMMUNICATING WITH THE TEEN-AGER

To insure an open line of communication with your teen-ager, re-main an attractive personality—one with whom it is rewarding to maintain a relationship. All you have to do to qualify is: stay in good physical shape; be competent at your own job; avoid a blaming orientation; act and be a strong but not overwhelming personality; have a good sense of humor; maintain a strong identity as husband or wife, father or mother; be firm in your decisions and emotional interests.

Taken as a whole, that list probably excludes about 90 percent of us. But the more of these objectives we can achieve, the easier communication will be.

In plain talk, why would anyone, especially a teen-ager, want to take orders or even suggestions from an unattractive personality? Your employees will if you are a boss—because you are in control of their destinies. But such is not the case with your teen-ager, who is pushed from within by an exceedingly intense need to be free even if it means giving up his accustomed standard of living, which means nothing to him anyway because he has probably never been without it and never had to work for it.

If we yield to the temptation to become naggers and complainers, instead of leaders, we will lose communication with those over whom we have no direct control. While we may still control the very physical survival of our youngest and even those thirteen or fourteen years old, things will be different with those fifteen, sixteen, seventeen. These young adults will learn that they do not really need us, that they could, if they had to, survive on their own. In actuality, they may be at least partially dependent on us. But because they are *less* dependent, they demand more of those who would lead them. With older children, allegiance must be freely given; it cannot be demanded. We must earn respect and not try to induce it with physical force—or appeasement.

If you look back over the opening list in this section, you will see that nowhere does it suggest you "get down to their level," give in, bribe, appease, or try to "understand" in the sense of go-along-with-what-is-wanted-even-though-it's-wrong.

One stays a worthy identification figure by being a happy, productive, loving, secure person with a philosophy of life that, if not perfect, is at least not too full of inconsistencies. In this way, even if the teen-ager does not agree with you, he at least has a rather clear idea of what it is he doesn't agree with. Teen-age rebellions are most aimless, diffuse, and violent when they are directed against a power structure lacking clarity or definition. Honest understanding, and genuine compromise—at no one's vital expense —are possible only so long as both sides understand the issues. This is unhappily not the case in the current society.

Not that complete clarity or satisfying compromise would be possible in a youth *vs.* establishment fight anyway. Teen-agers want and need a fight—a fight to put psychological distance between themselves and those from whom they wish to separate. They must put aside dependency needs; this is not easy. To overcome their own unconscious reluctance to leave the adults on whom they have depended for love, guidance, and protection, they must produce battles. By imagining they face insoluble differences, they can give themselves a motive to back away.

The harder we adults have made it for them to back away by not encouraging independence, the more violent must these disputes be. The same violence is bred if the adult establishment shows too much confusion within its own ranks. For then a certain blood lust is added to the picture: conscious and unconscious grievances, real and imagined, which would have stayed below the surface under less confused conditions, arise to the top and overflow. In the next chapter, on age sixteen and beyond, we will cover in more detail the issue of the generation gap. For now, we are concerned with methods of communication.

When you are in a discussion with a teen-ager, know your facts. There are numerous publications, many put out by the United States government, on drugs, alcohol, and the like. Your son or daughter will snow you, often with authoritatively stated incorrect facts, if you lack facts for rebuttal. So be prepared to cite figures and data. They are impressive and hard to argue with.

Nevertheless, be sure to *understate*, not *overstate*, your position. In fact, begin any discussion by paying very careful attention to what your teen-ager is saying. Recognize all that is right in his argument. Concede what is wrong on your side. *Ask many questions about his position—and do it honestly.* This will show him you really care about what he is trying to say. *The more respect you give his position, the more he will give yours.* Many parents lose the battle before it has begun by being as dogmatic and unlistening as their teen-agers who at least have the excuse that they need a fight.

And don't worry that winning an issue will deprive your teen-ager of his needed opportunity to rebel. There will be enough areas of honest disagreement. Your job is to keep these issues at a level that avoids violence and self-defeating behavior on the part of the teen-ager.

The family council will be a great aid, especially if you remember foundation skill 1, communicating without blame.

As we pointed out, the very formality of the family council gives teen-agers the psychological protection or "distance" they require to risk interaction. The more the two sides are in conflict, the more important this distance. It allows communication to continue in situations where it would otherwise be impossible.

Don't worry about the formality of the council becoming a total way of life: the council is, hopefully, not the only time you will be together.

DATING

The "correctness" of dating behavior depends on individual and family values. There is no correct age at which a child should begin dating. It depends on the degree of common sense. It also depends on what a teen-ager means by "dating" when he asks permission to indulge. Most of the boy and girl parties now in fashion for barely pubertal children are actually a matter of the girls gathering in one corner of the room to giggle, while the boys gather in another to brag and show off. Very few "boy and girl" things go on. Of course, this is not invariably the case. You must know your own child here.

Specify do's and don'ts, but avoid trying to judge personalities. Instead of telling your child whom she may date, tell her rather what the rules are: what time to arrive home, who are permissible drivers, etc.

Sexual play is again a matter of individual family values, but parents should learn to differentiate real issues—things truly hurtful to the child—from unreal issues—things that merely displease the parents or do not fit parental mythologies. For example, masturbation cannot hurt a child, although if done compulsively it may require investigation, as would any other compulsion. But an illegitimate pregnancy or promiscuity *may* hurt a child. Hence we would take a firm stand on these issues and emphasize them in setting limits.

THE UNDESIRABLE FRIEND

One of the saddest roles for a parent to assume is that of judge and jury for his child's friends. Very often, as the kids will tell you, we are in no position to do the judging. Unless the friend has a police record for something serious (not campus protest) or is a known and proven user of the more serious drugs (speed, the hallucinogens, opium products), you may find yourself judging him undesirable on very subjective bits of evidence—hair length or dirtiness of feet—and you may misjudge as antisocial many kids who are just kooky or having a hard time shaking off their childhoods.

Stick to council-generated rules to set up and maintain safe standards; avoid judging people about whom you possess no evidence. In other words, instead of saying, "I don't want you to drive with Jimmy," say, "You may not drive with unsafe drivers," and define those as drivers who rack up numerous tickets on their cars or those you have seen driving unsafely. If Jimmy happens to fall into this category, he is one of the persons with whom your child may not drive. *But approach the problem via the issues, not the personalities.* This may sound tricky, but it isn't. For it really *is* the issues that matter.

Another family-council-generated rule may be: you may not associate with users of the serious drugs. By limiting the restriction to serious drug users, you will show your knowledge of differences between drugs, and you will have acknowledged that not all drug users are unsafe companions. But remember to know your facts before you speak.

Since a good many users of the softer drugs, like marijuana, do in fact go on to the hard ones, you may eventually have to exclude friends who at first were sanctioned. Your youngsters should understand this.

Excluding a child from your own child's company is not always possible. Exclusions are enforceable only with young or very tractable teen-agers. And since it is a cardinal part of being a good and effective leader never to lay down an unenforceable rule, you will have to handle things differently with older children over whom your degree of parental control is small. When dealing with an unenforceable situation, tell the teen-ager that you are *not* going to command him but rather to *ask for* his cooperation.

SMOKING

If you feel strongly about your teen-ager smoking, tell him so. Although you cannot command him not to smoke because you cannot watch him all day, you can be firm: "I feel very strongly that I don't want you to smoke. Now I know I can't follow you around and force you not to, but I can tell you this is very important to me and I *hope* very much you will not do it. I feel strongly enough about it so that I will never give you permission to smoke in my presence or anywhere I can stop you."

Parents who say they would rather have their child smoke in front of them than behind their backs are stupid. Either they are for smoking or against it. They might as well say, "I'd rather you use opium in front of me than behind my back." Whether the child does it in front of you or behind you, it hurts him terribly.

Don't equivocate: make up your mind and then tell your child you will do all you can to enforce your beliefs on these crucial issues.

DRUGS

There are some things so serious that you must lay down rules you realize you cannot enforce completely. Drug usage falls into this category in our home.

Our position on drugs is this: "You may not use them, you may not experiment with them, you may not associate with people who sell them. You may not even associate with anyone who uses the hard drugs. There are no exceptions. We will do whatever we have to to enforce this rule. If you force us, we will even search your clothes and lock you in the house." This is indeed a hard position; it mirrors our feeling that the issue is serious. Both of us have worked with dozens of kids whose troubles were transformed by drug use from what would have been standard cases into nightmares. Hard drugs may not cause problems but they can make solvable problems unsolvable.

No matter what studies your teen-ager may cite, we contend drugs are dangerous. We have seen too many serious cases to doubt this.

The hard drugs are easy to prove dangerous. The situation is more complex with marijuana. Studies show it is not physically addicting. But our experience shows it may be psychologically addicting. And it is also a step-up drug. The psychological step between nothing and marijuana is much bigger than that between marijuana and something else. Once the first step has been taken, the second step is easy. Marijuana may not have been a step-up drug in the past. We suspect such was the case *because in the past there was nothing readily available to step up to*. The situation is grossly different now. Even our junior high schools abound with drug supplies.

To be quite honest, marijuana is *not* dangerous to everyone. A good many of the kids who use it do not seem to suffer because of it, and even some of those who do go on to the hard drugs realize their mistake and either go off drugs completely or go back to marijuana only. In spite of these concessions, we still do not sanction its use or that of any other drug. The risks are too high, and as yet there is no way to predict those individuals whose bio-neuro-psychological systems will tolerate continued drug abuse. Until such time as this is possible, there is no sense in adding drugs to the list of already available sanctioned killers such as tobacco and driver licenses granted on physical driving ability rather than judgment.

ANTISOCIAL BEHAVIOR

There is no single cause of antisocial behavior, and no single answer to its problems. Some causes will require solutions at a societal level, others at a family and individual level. Such behavior can be looked at as caused either by shared social values, by a build-up of intense drives, or by a faulty "braking" system. Of course, some antisocial behavior springs from the simultaneous operation of some or all of these factors.

Behavior based on shared cultural values: Sometimes a culture chooses to sanction violence, as, for example, under conditions of war. We do not label violence antisocial if it is committed in the name of national security. If a group has convinced itself that it pursues justice, it will commit anything, including violence, in its name. (The fact that some opposing group thinks *it* pursues justice does not seem to matter.) This "sanctioned" violence is not the same as that committed, for example, by a pugnacious teen-ager who looks for a way to revenge his hatred of authority (although one could make a good argument out of some of the similarities between the two situations).

Behavior based on irrationally intense drives: Antisocial behavior results when an aggressive motor force becomes stronger than the set of brakes that would contain them. Irrationally intense drives can be generated either by organic pathology or by false ideas which cause an individual to perceive danger when in fact none exists or convince him he desperately needs something he cannot have. He becomes frustrated, which in turn generates aggression. The "cure" for this type of aggression may be medical or psychological. A treatment aiming to reduce intense drives may be combined with one that seeks simultaneously to build up the braking system.

Behavior based on a weak system of "brakes": Here we may deal with psychopathic behavior—behavior caused not by an overabundance of intense aggressive drives but rather by a complete or nearly complete absence of those factors that would soften, divert, or somehow modify the aggressive impulses that do exist. Brakes are based both on attitudes and on an intact nervous system. The braking attitudes are those of social concern: empathy for others, an ability to project oneself into the identities of intended victims. Faulty braking systems can also be caused by organic pathology which may make it hard for an individual to develop a consistent set of social beliefs with which to modify aggressive urges.

All forms of antisocial behavior fit into these categories.

It is not easy to find answers to the problems posed by antisocial behavior, although it *is* possible to spend a lot of time barking up wrong trees instead of facing the real issues. For example, it seems fairly clear that poor salaries, poor housing, and so on, cannot by themselves cause violence. Ghetto violence is caused by frustration, and frustration is psychological. It is caused by a disparity between what a person thinks he has and what he thinks he would like to have. The greater the disparity the greater the frustration, and hence the greater the potential fuel for violence. All of these concepts are psychological. Hence we can find no cheap answer to violence simply by spending more money on housing. This doesn't mean we shouldn't spend that money. We should, but for the right reason: out of a sense of care for our fellow humans.

But our real job is to *reduce frustration*—and frustration is definitional. The problem is a psychological one, and money will not by itself solve it. There are many poor people who are not violent, and many wealthy people who are. *Any* person is free to feel frustrated and hence primed for violence; the privilege is not limited to the poor. All one has to do is decide he wants more than he has the capacity to get, and that he *ought* to have what he wants. This is not to say that there is no difference between an act of violence committed in the name of true deprivation and one committed for superfluities. But frustration remains the cause.

A spoiled child *feels he needs* overabundances of supplies to survive. His need for supplies grows irrationally intense—stronger than his braking system can contain and too much for anyone to satisfy. The more his mother gives the more the child wants. This is a prime example of how attitudes generate frustration. The child may attempt to bully to get what he has been led to believe (irrationally) he needs.

Some children in committing antisocial acts are acting out the unconscious wishes of their parents. It requires a trained eye to spot and remedy this. And some of the most extreme forms of violent aggression are committed by males who fear they harbor feminine attitudes with which they cannot cope.

Antisocial behavior takes many forms: stealing, running away, fire setting—homicide. But there is no single causal thread running through these different acts. Every case must be considered on its own.

Any and all children who commit persistent acts of an antisocial nature should receive medical and psychological evaluations. From a psychological standpoint, the main treatment method is to change or modify the attitudes in whose name the aggression is called forth. On the home front, this would involve all the foundation skills and the family council. Try to determine one or more of the underlying causes at work: Is the child spoiled? Does he perceive danger when none exists? Does he feel you do not give him enough?

At the family council review what is happening. Use skill 4, acknowledgments, to help him see what he is doing. Encourage him to set up a system to guide himself. Tell him if he won't, you will.

If the child is spoiled, interpret this: "You seem happy only when you are somehow getting things."

If the lad perceives danger where none exists, point this out: "You react as though you must defend yourself when in fact no one is attacking you, and you're not in any danger."

In persistent cases, seek professional help.

19
Age Sixteen and Beyond

Most of the important guidance work has been done by the time the child is sixteen. Parental control is minimal now; it has been weakening for some time. By now physical enforcement of rules has become difficult—in some cases, impossible.

When dependency or other neurotic conflicts are intense in either parent or child, any relationship between parent and teen-ager may be well-nigh impossible. Indeed in some cases a relationship may remain out of the question forever, or at least until such time as the teen-ager becomes a parent himself and finally realizes what his own parents were up against. Remember that children do not—cannot—understand their parents until they themselves have children. Only a parent can realize how another parent feels.

Parents of children sixteen and beyond must remain sounding boards, voices of reason, gentle goodhumored nonsarcastic hecklers, and sources of both a coherent point of view and affection.

The issues on which they must take firm stands are few but still exist: drugs, crime, inappropriate pregnancies. How far this list should extend is an individual matter.

The carrying out of at least some family responsibilities must be insisted upon. If both parents stand firm, observe skill 1 and use the council, this should be a *gradually* realizable goal, even in "severe" cases.

Our own personal belief is that parents should never desert their offspring—no matter what. By this we do not mean they should condone everything. We just mean that even if the young adult does something which the parents think wrong but cannot control—makes a poor marriage or quits school—the parents should still maintain an emotional relationship with their offspring. If one of our children should marry someone about whom we harbored serious doubts, we would say, "We think you are making a very bad mistake—but we will not desert you." Inside, we might be hurt and depressed for a time, but we would recover. We could never disown our adult children as some tragically vindictive parents do.

THE GENERATION GAP

Youth demands to know why adults allow inequities to exist which they presume can be cured by mere willpower and/or money, and why adults are so materialistic and seemingly hypocritical. Adults want to know why youth cannot gain perspective on today's plight and realize that some inequities have to do with human failings rather than with the failings of a particular generation. Adults also want to know what has happened to respect for authority and meaningful preparation for the future.

Some social commentators attribute the difficulty to the fact that we live in a time of rapid change. It is impossible to prepare for the future since it changes so rapidly, and so one must live in the present. Consequently, the idea of accumulating wealth and working hard while young to enjoy a restful period later has lost much of its appeal—or at least it might seem so. Interest has shifted to the inner world—an aspect of the here and now—and to interhuman relations, also part of the here and now.

But rapid change is only one of a number of forces at work. Nowhere can the effects of these forces be seen so clearly as in relation to the concept of authority. One need not be a social scholar to note that traditional forms of authority are no longer respected. We see this in the relationship of teen-agers to their professors, their schools, their political leaders—indeed to their government.

There is no longer a willingness to accept a pronouncement as valid merely because it issues from some traditional source of authority.

Loss of Authority

All of the following factors produce changes in attitudes toward traditional forms of authority.

1. Never before has the idea that truth is relative found such *emotional acceptance* as today. The idea of relativity is not new to philosophers; the universal acceptance of the idea is. And once the idea of a single truth is weakened, so too is the idea of authority. For possession of the truth is what grants an authority its power. And if there are no stable truths, then there can be no stable authority.

    In bygone years if an adult were to tell a child to do something a certain way, and then list his reasons, the child may not have complied. But if he didn't, it was because he would not accept that *particular* order. He would not question its philosophical foundation. Today, if you tell a youngster to believe and hence do something, he is likely to say to you, "That's your way of looking at things—not my way." In other words, youth does not merely reject particular parental suggestions; they reject our whole way of evaluating activities. The idea of absolute authority is hard to maintain within a system that sees the "truth" as varying with the situation.

    There are few central values today about which everyone agrees. There are fewer commitments, less dedication to long-term, immutable ideals. When there is no way to agree on definite values, all behaviors tend to be deemed acceptable.

2. The gradual spread and distortion of some of Freud's ideas

have weakened respect for authority. People have misunderstood Freud in a number of ways. First, in the difference between understanding or explaining why a person does a certain thing and deciding how accountable he should be held for the act. The fact that we can explain *why* a person does something tells nothing about how accountable he should be held. Because psychological science uses deterministic concepts does not necessarily mean a person has no control over his destiny. Much confused thinking seems to have crept into our ways of dealing with crime; for example, the belief that understanding why a man may have committed a crime yields some clear-cut notion as to what, if anything, should be done to him. Today's youth uses fallacious reasoning to come to the conclusion that since all men are just satisfying blind needs over which they have no control, anything goes.

Second, since within the Freudian system it is possible to explain the man who does social good with the same set of concepts one would use to explain the man of evil, the fallacious conclusion has been drawn that the two men are of equal value. The Christian saints used to be looked up to as representing a high moral force. Today's view might see in them more neurosis than saintliness. It is hard to impress our youth with examples of good behavior. They may answer with "He was only doing what he had to do."

3. Authority concepts are undergoing change because of our emphasis on independence. We teach our children to question authority. If a child hears something he cannot accept, he is literally taught to question and challenge. Most of us see this type of behavior as highly desirable, and it is, especially in our type of society. But the gain in individual freedom is purchased at a price, as is every other social gain. The price is a psychological "fallout" with which we have not yet begun to deal. New solutions must be found to deal with this fallout—this psychological aftermath. The family council, backed by the foundation skills, is one such attempt.

4. Sons are encouraged to outdo their fathers rather than to fol-

low in their footsteps. This adds one more burden to the notion
of authority. We do not want our children to follow the same
paths we took; we want them to do better.

Also, there is less use of the apprentice system which encouraged devotion to a single male authority.

Other Factors in the Gap

1. There is a lack of perspective among the youth in the United
   States that results from the way history is taught in our
   schools, especially in the early grades, as though it began in
   1776. This lack of perspective produces historical naïveté.
2. Teen-agers always believe themselves motivated by greater concern for the common good than are their fathers. And since
   they have never had to make important decisions on running
   a complex society, especially on engendering an economic
   system that would be deemed just by everyone, they see solutions simplistically: "Why don't we all share what we have?"
   Of course it is much easier to suggest sharing what one has
   when one has either nothing or very little. Basing their solutions to the problems of running a society's economy on what
   they learned from a three-day stay at a musical event (where
   all the important work of providing food, medical attention,
   and so on was done by outsiders) they imagine the same system
   will work with society at large. But people remain warm, loving, sharing, all-peaceful, and content only so long as no important decisions have to be made. Picture what would happen
   as soon as agreement was needed as to where the wells should
   be dug, where the cesspools installed, who should do what.
   Communes work only so long as their members are healthy,
   productive, and capable of group decision-making. And an-
   archy, which some of today's youth mistake for freedom, is
   relatively easy to tolerate only if one has nothing to lose.
3. Increasing amounts of leisure time may contribute negatively
   to overall psychological stability. There is some question as to
   how much leisure people can safely handle. Most people, ra-

tionally, or irrationally, derive their sense of self-worth from accomplishment. A certain kind of potential-for-violence can overtake people who are not busy, who cannot derive a sense of self-worth from accomplishment, and who are cut off more and more from the final products to which they contribute.

By camping out, close to the basics, our family experienced a feeling reported by others—a feeling of well-being, happiness, and potency. This feeling cannot be explained by the mere absence of pressure, as this can be achieved on all types of vacations. Nor can it be explained fully by the notion of a masculine conquering of nature, since women experience the feeling, too.

It takes a long time to gather firewood and to prepare food for outdoor cooking. Washing and caring for the body and clothing add more time. In other words, most of the day is taken up with basics. There is little time to indulge in highly abstract, negative thinking. It is interesting that even philosophers with their heads up in the clouds often make sure they lead basically simple lives. This is typically explained as their desire not to waste time. However, perhaps these philosophers (like many Zen masters) discovered that a very simple basic life contributes to mental health. It is an open question in our urban society how much a human being can depart from these day-filling, yet stimulating routines and still maintain a healthy, nonviolent balance.

4. Our educational systems are irrelevant in many instances. Many of us are being trained for technological lives. Little emphasis is placed on learning how to get along with others or on how to have a satisfactory sexual experience and raise a family. Yet these are things almost all of us will be doing. It seems we spend the lion's share of schooltime teaching things that occupy people relatively little, and hardly any time at all teaching skills that will be used daily. Almost all people will interact with others, copulate, marry, and have children. Yet those are the things schools do not bother with, apparently presuming parents should teach these skills. The divorce rate, venereal disease

rate, and the number of illegitimate children suggest things could perhaps be done better.

5. Lewis S. Feuer in his article "Conflict of Generations," emphasizes the id-like irrational nature of generation conflicts, reminding us of the roles of complex unconscious sources. Such wellsprings of rebellion are hard to touch with reason, for unlike a labor rebellion, which derives from specific grievances, student rebellions are intense emotions searching for a cause. They have a vague, ill-defined character about them. Feuer feels that youth will *always* choose violent methods of seeking redress, even when other alternatives exist, presumably because of the repressed hatred dependent persons feel toward those on whom they are dependent.

SOME SUGGESTIONS

No one really wants to "cure" the generation gap, since it is a bio-psychosocial necessity. Individual identity could not crystallize unless it had something to push against when forming itself. A plastic, semiformed substance could not solidify unless it had something firm to press itself against: a mushy "something" would not do. Parents who lack a coherent sense of identity cannot help younger beings find themselves. Mushiness breeds unpredictability. When a youth encounters a vague sense of identity in the adult against whom he had hoped to find himself, he responds chaotically—with either diffuse violence, or laziness, or a lack of clear values. Such is part of the problem we face today.

But if we cannot "cure" the generation gap we still need to do something: we need to deal with the psychological fallout of the problems of our age. One thing needed is a way to reestablish communication with youth. Even young teen-agers, thirteen to fifteen years of age, imitating their older brothers and sisters, balk now at traditional family responsibilities.

A method, democratic, yet sound from a parental point of

view, is needed. The family council *plus* the four foundation skills is one possibility. The sooner (in terms of the age of the children) the system is used, the better.

Now for other suggestions:

1. Teen-agers have a need to argue. Argue with them. Keep smiling inside—if not openly.
2. Teen-agers have a need to disagree with your points of view. Don't knock yourself out to win approval and acceptance of all your views, except on crucial issues.
3. In setting limits, do not set your advance guard too far front. Many parents, in attempting to stave off antisocial behavior, may not let a child go out at all, or in fearing drug use will forbid him to wear long hair. The reasoning seems to be "If I give in on this point, if I let him have long hair, the next step is inevitable—he'll use drugs."

    This reasoning is usually not valid, and it invites the teen-ager to reject *all* your ideas. An anxious woman once called our radio program and asked what she could do about a thirteen-year-old girl who opened the door of the house at one o'clock in the morning after some stranger had knocked. In the course of the conversation, we asked the mother to give some examples of the limits imposed on her daughter. She said, "Well —not to open the door to strangers. . . . Not to walk alone at night after dark. . . . Not to talk on the phone to any teen-agers." . . . We stopped her at this point. Her list was a dead giveaway. She mixed sensible restrictions with ridiculous ones. Under such conditions, the teen-ager rejects the entire package, unable to make sense of it. If you overdo your restrictions, you risk total rejection.
4. If your teen-age child is given some medical or dental orders to follow, let the professional impress him with the importance of obeying. Teen-agers find it easier to accept limits from authority figures outside the family.
5. Do not be offended when your teen-ager does not want to

spend much time with you. "I can't understand that kid—here we are going to the seashore and he'd rather hang with his same old gang of friends."

6. Your teen-ager will frequently accuse you, perhaps violently, of being overprotective. This attitude, solicitous overconcern, is more than offensive to a teen-ager: it is threatening. His reaction to it will not be logical. He may explode, really curse you out. We have found one verbal answer better than others: "Since the beginning of time parents have been worried—perhaps overworried—about their kids. What has been going on already for ten thousand or more years isn't going to stop right here with me. Look somewhere else for pioneers."

This puts the worry in perspective, and points out that the teen-ager in question is not the first to have been overprotected. Further, it introduces some humor into what could be a bitter confrontation.

ONE LAST WORD

Please remember that the ideas presented here work best when used as a whole. The family council idea will work on its own—but will be far more effective if all four foundation skills are used along with it: communicating without blame, setting appropriate limits, encouraging independence, and making proper acknowledgments.

The more disturbed your child is to begin with, the longer it will take to get results. So do not be upset if gains are not manifest at once, especially if your child has been highly provocative and frequently out of control. When he finds himself confronted with a firm parental front, when he can no longer evoke the negative emotion to which he has become addicted, when he realizes you intend to hold firm to your limits, and when he finds that you actually understand him as shown in your acknowledgments, he *isn't* going to be happy. He doesn't want you to be nice to him —at least not too nice. He doesn't want your positive emotion;

he doesn't know what to do with it. He is used to negative emotion. And he definitely does not want to be understood—at least the sick part of him doesn't. Without knowing why, he will feel threatened—as if he is being asked to give up something vital. He will fight back. But in spite of himself he will feel better. You will observe the well-known Ping-Pong improvement effect. He will feel better for longer periods of time. But his negative episodes may be more intense, as he tries to push you back into the same old patterns with which he felt comfortable. It will take him awhile to adjust to the new ways. But if you persist, he *will* adjust. Eventually you will notice that although he still has some out-of-control episodes, they are less frequent. And in just a little while longer, you will notice the episodes do not last very long, and are not quite so intense as before. He can yield on a point or two without feeling crushed.

Remember: the criterion of improvement is the frequency of good (or poor) days, not the mere presence or absence of negative episodes.

The genesis of children's and adults' problems is not yet completely clear. Conflicts—situations in which a person is pushed to accomplish two mutually exclusive goals—seem a part of the cause. Subtle bio-neuro-psychological disabilities seem further implicated—at least in some cases. But no matter where future paths in the healing sciences lead—to new medicines, to other forms of behavioral control, to confronting inner worlds existentially and/or psychoanalytically—firm parental systems will be needed.

We have not yet begun to realize the therapeutic benefits of firm, insightful, nonblaming, acknowledging parental systems. The present book offers one such system.

Bibliography

ARNOLD, MAGDA B., *Emotion and Personality*. Vols. I and II. New York, Columbia University Press, 1960.

———, ed., *The Nature of Emotion*. Baltimore, Penguin, 1968.

Better Homes and Gardens Baby Book. Des Moines, Iowa, Bantam, 1965.

CARDANO, GIROLAMO, "On Himself and His Life." In J. B. Ross and Mary McLaughlin, eds., *The Portable Renaissance Reader*. New York, Viking Press, 1953, pp. 512–524.

DAS, BHAGAVAN, *The Science of Emotions*, fourth ed. Adyar, Madras, India, Theosophical Publishing House, 1953.

ELLIS, ALBERT, *Reason and Emotion in Psychotherapy*. New York, Lyle Stuart, 1962.

ERIKSON, ERIK, *Childhood and Society*, rev. ed. New York, W. W. Norton, 1968.

———, *Identity: Youth and Crisis*. New York, W. W. Norton, 1968.

———, *Young Man Luther*. New York, W. W. Norton, 1958.

FEUER, LEWIS S., "Conflict of Generations." *Saturday Review*, January 18, 1969, p. 53.

FOLSOM, J. K., "Sexual and Affectional Functions of the Family," in A. Ellis and A. Abarbanel, eds., *The Encyclopedia of Sexual Behavior*. New York, Hawthorn, 1961, pp. 392–411.

ILG, FRANCES L. and Ames, Louise Bates, *Child Behavior*. New York, Harper and Row, 1966.

REIK, THEODOR, *Of Love and Lust*. New York, Evergreen Books, 1949. (Reik's original work, A *Psychologist Looks at Love* appeared much earlier.)

SPOCK, BENJAMIN, *Baby and Child Care*, rev. ed. New York, Duell, Sloan and Pearce, 1968.

Index

About the Authors

Barry Bricklin, Ph.D., is a research assistant professor of psychiatry in psychology at the Hahnemann Medical College of Philadelphia. He was formerly an instructor in psychology and an associate in the Department of Psychiatry at the Jefferson Medical College of Philadelphia. He has been a consultant to the Walter Reed Army Hospital Research Center, to the E. I. duPont de Nemours Co., to the New York Academy of Medicine, and to the Columbia Broadcasting System. Dr. Bricklin is past president of the Philadelphia Society for Projective Techniques, and past president of the Philadelphia Society of Clinical Psychologists. He is coauthor of a book on a new projective test, and has published articles, among others, on prognosis in schizophrenia, marital compatibility, the psychology of affiliation, the intercultural use of the Rorschach test, and Ethiopian children. Dr. Bricklin has worked with mildly and seriously disturbed adults and children as a psychodiagnostician and psychotherapist in private practice and in institutional settings.

Patricia M. Bricklin, Ph.D., is on the faculty of the Department of Psychiatry at the Hahnemann Medical College and is consultant to the Parkway Day School. Formerly she was psychological consultant to the Valley Day School for children with learning and adjustment problems, and to the Bucks County Public Schools. Dr. Bricklin has lectured in psychology at Temple University and was supervisor of the diagnostic division of the university's reading clinic. She has been a consultant to the learning disability clinic at Jefferson Medical College, has conducted workshops on reading disabilities in public and private schools, and taught in-service reading courses for elementary and high school teachers. For five years she taught children with severe learning and adjustment problems at the Matthews School, of Baltimore, Maryland, and Fort Washington, Pennsylvania. She has also served as a consultant to the Columbia Broadcasting System.

Dr. Patricia Bricklin is past president of the Philadelphia Society for Projective Techniques. She has published articles on the diagnosis and treatment of children with learning disabilities and related emotional disorders, as well as the counseling of parents.

Among the things on which she has cooperated in producing with her husband are a book on underachievement, *Bright Child—Poor Grades,* two sons, Brian and Scott, and a daughter, Carol.

The Bricklins were hosts of a popular radio show on psychology for four years in Philadelphia and are currently hosts of a television show in that area.